Voices of the Veiled Age

The Forgotten Chronicles of Zubayda bint Jaʻfar

by

Fatima Daulati

Translated by

Sara Brown

Copyright © 2026 by Lantern Publications

Originally published by Jamkaraan Publications under the title من بر می‌گردم

All rights reserved. No part of this publication may be reproduced, distributed, or transmitted in any form or by any means, including photocopying, recording, or other electronic or mechanical methods, without the prior written permission of the publisher, except in the case of brief quotations embodied in critical reviews and certain other noncommercial uses permitted by copyright law. For permission requests, write to the publisher, addressed "Attention: - Permissions- Voices of the veiled age" at the email address below.

Lantern Publications
info@lanternpublications.com
www.lanternpublications.com
Ordering Information:
Quantity sales. Special discounts are available on quantity purchases by corporations, associations, and others. For details, contact the distributor at the address below.

Shī'a Books Australia
www.shiabooks.com.au
info@shiabooks.com.au

A catalogue record for this book is available from the National Library of Australia

ISBN- 978-1-922583-72-7

First Edition

In the Name of God,

The Most Compassionate, the Most Merciful

Prayers of God's Peace and Blessings

In keeping with the Islamic practice of showing respect for the name of God, and sending prayers of God's peace and blessings whenever the name of His blessed Prophet, Lady Fātima, and the Twelve Imams is mentioned, as well as for asking God to hasten the reappearance of the Lord of the Age on the Earthly plane, one or more of the following Arabic symbols have been employed throughout the text. They are repeated for their great rewards.

 Used exclusively after the name of God, meaning "the Sublimely Exalted", or, as a prayer, "[May His name be] Sublimely Exalted".

 Used exclusively after the name of the Prophet, meaning "May the peace and blessings of God be unto him and unto [the purified and inerrant members of] his family"

 Used for any of the Twelve Imams or past prophets of God, meaning "May God's peace be unto him".

 Used for two or more of the Twelve Imams or past prophets of God, meaning "May God's peace be unto them".

 Used for Lady Fātima, meaning "May God's peace be unto her".

 Used for a plurality of the Fourteen Immaculates, meaning "May God's peace be unto them all collectively".

 Used for the Lord of the Age (the Twelfth Imam), meaning "May God hasten the advent of his noble person".

Publisher's Foreword

History is often narrated through the actions of rulers and the rise and fall of empires. Yet Islamic tradition has always known that the accurate measure of an age is not found in its palaces, but in those who recognised truth when it was dangerous to do so, and who stood beside it when silence would have been safer.

This novel is rooted in a narration attributed to Imam Jaʿfar al-Ṣādiq ﷺ, preserved in Shia biographical and ethical literature, in which he names women of extraordinary faith and steadfastness: Umm Ayman (Barakah), Sumayya bint Khayyat, Qanwa bint Rushayd al-Hijrī, Umm Khalid, Siyana the believer, and Zubayda bint Jaʿfar. These women are not remembered as symbolic ideals but as historical exemplars, individuals whose lives bore witness to divine truth under immense political, social, and personal pressure. The authenticity of the spiritual legacy they represent is firmly embedded within the Shia tradition.

What unites these women is not status, circumstance, or ease. Some lived in poverty, others in splendour; some were persecuted openly, others lived within the courts of tyrants. What unites them is an unwavering attachment to the true guides of Islam, the Maʿṣūm Prophets and Imams, and an innate, deeply rooted need to remain close to them, to protect them, and to preserve their message when it was most threatened. In Shia theology, proximity to the Maʿṣūm is not merely devotional; it is formative. It shapes conscience, clarifies moral vision, and demands responsibility. The courage these women displayed did not arise from temperament or circumstance, but from certainty in whom they stood beside.

This work powerfully challenges the persistent misconception that women in Islam were passive or defined solely by the men around them. Islamic history, when read honestly, records women who remained morally independent even when bound by marriage to men of cruelty and power. Their faith did not depend on the righteousness of their husbands, nor did their courage require authority or safety. They spoke when speech carried a cost. They remained loyal when loyalty invited punishment. Their steadfastness stands as a testament to the spiritual agency Islam affords women, not in theory, but in lived reality.

The inspiration of this book extends to both women and men. For women, it affirms that faith grants moral authority independent of circumstance or permission. For men, it offers a humbling reminder that spiritual greatness has never been the exclusive domain of power, rank, or gender. The guardianship of truth has always rested with those willing to suffer for it.

What elevates this novel further is its craft. Written with restraint, depth, and emotional intelligence, the prose is lyrical without excess and uncompromising in its ethical clarity. History is rendered not as a distant chronicle, but as a lived experience, allowing the reader to feel the weight of palaces, the hush of prisons, and the quiet heroism of belief passed from one generation to the next.

Voices of the Veiled Age is more than a historical novel. It is an act of remembrance and fidelity, to memory, to truth, and to the sacred lineage of guidance these women loved and protected. In restoring their voices, this book restores a vital truth: that the defence of Islam has always been carried, in no small part, by women whose courage was born from devotion to the Ma'ṣūmīn and whose legacy continues to illuminate the path of faith.

Lantern Publications
Sydney, Australia.
January 2026

Voices of a veiled age

Voices of a veiled age

1

It's been a week since I died. Right here, in this very room where he first reached for my hand, where he leaned in close and whispered, "You are the lady of my heart." Under this same roof, he saw our son Amin for the first time. I can still see him fall to the floor in prostration, tears in his eyes, overcome with joy.

I look at myself in the mirror. A tall woman, her face is pale like snow that hasn't been touched. Her eyes, neither bloodshot nor teary, just... still. I've had a week to cry. A week to face myself. Seven days that have stretched like a thousand years, bitter and slow. Now that I've given up on everything and I'm ready to leave, I just want a trace of hope, a sliver of light. Something like the sun, to thaw this frost in my chest. So maybe, just maybe, something in me can sprout again. Something green.

Voices of a veiled age

I look at the mirror once more. People think I died last week, the day I lost everything I once called mine. But they don't know the truth. The truth is, my life ended months ago, the day I learned my Imam had been martyred by his order. The man who was my husband. The father of my child. The man I once loved. How did I keep standing after that? How did I even keep breathing?

I reach up and unclasp the necklace around my neck, a gift from him on our wedding night. Last night, a messenger from the palace brought a command: The Commander of the Faithful, Harun al-Rashid, ordered me to leave behind all my gold, coins, and gowns, and to go. This necklace, once a symbol of love, now feels like a relic of a life I must abandon.

He has foolishly imagined. I will take nothing with me from this house and from him, not even this necklace. He gave it to me on our wedding night. He pulled it from a chest full of jewels and pearls. His breath warmed the skin at my neck as he whispered, "Your love is eternal in my heart, Zubayda." That sentence stayed with me deep in my soft and innocent heart, the heart of a seventeen-year-old girl who was still pure and without guile.

We were cousins. One day, like any other, he came to visit our grandfather. His thick eyebrows were furrowed, a crease between them. He was tense, and his long face looked more grown-up and manly than I'd ever seen before. He was talking nonstop, and every so often, he would stroke his thin beard. I don't know why I stayed there behind the curtain, looking him over from head to toe, once, then again. And suddenly it hit me like a bolt of lightning. It was sharp, electric, and impossible to ignore. My cheeks flushed. My ears burned hot. And when he finally left, it felt like he had taken a piece of me with him. I remember that day clearly. I had a strand of my hair wrapped around my finger and kept pulling at it. When my mother called out 'Zubayda,' it felt like something snapped inside me. I felt like a thief who had been caught. I thought Harun's image was stamped deep in the darkness of my eyes, and if my mother looked closely, she'd see the secret in my heart. But no one noticed. After that day, my heart beat a thousand times in an hour for him. Alone in my room, I whispered his name, Harun, and he became real. He rose like a wave in the air and clawed at my heart. Overwhelmed by a feeling I had no name for, I made wudu and prayed again and again, no matter the time.

In the midst of all the bustle of life in the Abbasid household, my grandfather Mansur was the one who truly understood how I felt those moods that swung from dreamy joy to sudden chaos. He had introduced me to poetry and storytelling when I was just three. And whenever the routines of life wore him down, he would say, 'Zubayda, read me a poem.' And I always did. But after that day, I began to see Harun in every line of poetry. My mind would soar towards a sky whose name I now knew: love.

Once, I was sitting next to my grandfather. My eyes were closed, and I was reading him poetry with boundless passion. I was lost in my own world, moving through each word, when suddenly he cut me off. 'Do you need something, Harun?' At the sound of his name, I flushed with heat. My face burned with embarrassment. I opened my eyes and saw him standing by the door. He was looking at me, his eyes smiling. I don't know how I got up and left my grandfather's room, but his sweet gaze stayed with me. That sweetness has stayed with me all these years. But somewhere deep in us, the foundation of my relationship with Harun cracked. I know where, I know how… going over these memories doesn't end, and it doesn't help. Remembering things that were once sweet but now feel like bitter poison only makes me more tired. Loving him was a mistake. I should have held on to my heart tighter. I should have stayed away from him. But…

I toss the necklace beside the earrings and bracelets. My gaze moves slowly around the corners of the room. The fire pits are still burning. The fountains are flowing. The ivy pots have taken the room's columns into their embrace. And on the table in the corner, the fruits sit in the basket, and the sweets sit quietly in the dish.

The crystal goblets sit on a red velvet tablecloth, and the decanter of saffron sherbet hasn't been touched in days. This room, this palace, this world all go on without me. Without Zubayda. Still standing. Still moving forward. Life goes on. Where do I belong in a world this bright, this full of colour? And one I had even before him, simply because I was the cherished daughter of the Abbasids. There was a time when I thought this dream had been promised to me. Now I know that life is waiting somewhere beyond these marble walls.

I tuck my small bundle under my arm and glance at Henna, at her soft, bright eyes. She's not one of Harun's possessions. She's my childhood playmate, the one who held my secrets long ago. It grew up in my hands and learned on my shoulder to constantly repeat, 'Zubayda, Zubayda.' When I lift its cage off the golden stand, it clings to the bars. Just as I once clung to the bars of this palace. A cage is still a cage. Does it matter if its bars are iron or marble, ruby and jade? I take the Qur'an wrapped in silk from the shelf. A mournful recitation echoes through the halls. The girls have gathered one last time. Their sad voices rise to send me off. It will be the last time I hear them read together.

Voices of a veiled age

I step toward the door, but my knees falter. I press the Quran against my chest. It's a keepsake. It carries his memory. When my circle of handmaids grew, I decided to teach them to read. We would gather in a large hall, where I recited, and they repeated. It didn't take long for our gathering to come to life. Every day we read the Quran, each of us one page.

When the voices of the girls blended, it felt as if I were standing in a garden filled with nightingales' song and the hum of bees. It was during those days that Harun summoned me and invited me into his royal retreat. The maidservants and guards cleared the path and bowed deeply as I passed. He stepped forward and placed this Quran in my hands. He rolled his onyx prayer beads between his fingers and whispered, 'A gift from Harun to the lady of his palace, Zubayda.' A Quran with a leather cover, a jade emblem, and pages scented with musk from the deer. He knew well how to keep up appearances and to present himself as a servant of God. But deceit and guile were always part of him. He would frown whenever he saw me reading the Quran alone. But when I spoke of reading it together with the girls, he suddenly became a lover of God's word.

The sound of their recitation has now faded. Once, it calmed my heart. I found comfort in knowing that amidst the palace's nightly revelries, I had kept the words of God alive. That I, too, read every day and reflected on the verses. But now it brings no joy. I walk back the path I came, kiss the Quran, and place it on the shelf. Harun's keepsakes must stay here. I must go somewhere untouched by memory.

My mother used to say two things in this world can break a person: memory and secrets. She was right. Wrestling with memories is no easy thing. It's torture. The kind that drags a soul toward ruin. You keep

Voices of a veiled age

noticing your mistakes and how naive you were, and a fire burns deep inside you... And secrets weigh on the chest until it can no longer breathe.

Secrets weigh heavily on the chest, crushing it. I believe no secret truly remains hidden forever; they only pile up like rubble on the heart of their owner, stabbing, rubbing salt in the wound, stealing sleep from the eyes and smiles from the lips. You thrash endlessly in fear without end. You hang suspended, like a half-dead branch clinging to a tree...

My mother used to say that the day a secret is revealed is the day its owner finds peace. The day the burden lifts.

She was right. Seven days ago, when I finally revealed my secret, I felt lighter. I push my thoughts aside. I must take hold of the reins of my heart, hurry, move my feet, open the door, endure the heavy gazes of the palace women, and with the camel driver waiting for me, set off for nowhere.

I reached for the door, but before I stepped out, I heard her voice.

"Lady, my lady! Where are you? What a disaster has fallen upon us!"

The voice presses into my ear, pushing aside the whispers of my heart. It's Haniya. Haniya has returned.

"My lady! Lady Zubayda ..."

How many months has it been since I last saw her? I don't know. Since she left, the days have dragged and the nights grown darker. When she was here, she was my confidante.

I open the door, ignoring the women standing to watch and Amin by my room's threshold. I see Haniya running down the marble corridor toward me, a black scarf wrapped around her head, her eyes red and her face pale and wilted.

"Haniya... you came? What happened? What's with your face? Speak, girl..."

"May I give my life for you, my lady! Hababeh is gone. She has left us."

"Hababeh... Hababeh... What is she saying? Am I dreaming? Is this a nightmare?"

Haniya stands in front of me and takes my hands. Her fingertips are ice cold. I don't want to believe what I'm hearing.

"What are you saying, Haniya? What do you mean?"

"Hababeh, dear Hababeh... she's gone. You saw yourself she wasn't well. As soon as we reached Medina, she got worse. The coughing wore her down. She kept coughing up blood. On the last night, she seemed fine, but... she went to sleep and never woke up."

Tears brim in my eyes. Truth, at times, is poison. And the truth of Hababeh's death, the one I had dreaded to even think about, now burns bitter in the depths of my soul. She had known her days were numbered. She knew she had no breath left to spare.

I draw Haniya into my arms. Her shoulders tremble, but I do not let my sorrow break. Out of the corner of my eye, I see a guard by the door signaling a maid to approach. The girl walks up quietly, bows, and says, "Lady Zubayda, they say you must leave soon. The camel driver is waiting."

I nod. Once, in this palace, Hababeh's words soothed my broken heart. Now, the news of her death, today, here, in the hallway of Al-Khuld Palace, is a sign that I must trust the path I've chosen.

I grip Haniya's arms and ask, "Did Hababeh seal her stone?"

Haniya wipes her tears with the back of her hand and nods. My heart settles.

"Will you come with me?"

"Where to, Lady Zubayda? Wherever you go, I will follow. I have no one but you…"

I avert my eyes from Haniya. The weight of their stares presses on me. I don't want their last memory of me to be that of a trembling woman. I don't want whispers of my weakness and confusion to echo through the palace long after I'm gone. I don't even want to be called *Lady* anymore. Being the lady of this palace means my hands are stained with the blood of the Imam. And now, as I stand here, all I want is to dye my hands with the blood of his killer.

Amin steps forward. I raise my hand to stop him. I clear my throat. I must speak.

"I am no longer lady Zubayda. I am only Zubayda, daughter of Jafar. The same Zubayda whom the Caliph Harun al-Rashid cast out of his palace. The camel driver should be waiting for me. I will leave within the hour. But first, I must go elsewhere. If this goes against your Caliph's will, tell him to order my arrest. I do not fear him."

The guard retreats. Amin comes closer and asks, "Where are you going, Mother? Why are you doing this?"

I don't answer. He's becoming like his father. I can see it written in the lines of his face.

The murmurs of the palace women rise around me. Haniya takes a step closer, looking at me with wide, questioning eyes. In her gaze, I see a thousand unspoken questions.

The day she left, I was still Harun's favorite, the lady of Al-Khuld Palace. But after her departure, after hearing Hababeh's words and making that decision, all the gardens and orchards of the city, this magnificent palace, and its long halls became a narrow, suffocating prison in my eyes. The towering trees, the red flowers, the fountains, and the melodious birds all of it felt like torture.

I no longer have any place in this palace. Hababeh's image does not leave my mind for a moment. I still see her, an old woman with a bent back and hazel eyes clouded like mist, who walked down this very hallway with the help of her cane and showed me that God's gaze is upon me.

Haniya holds my bundle in one hand and the henna cage in the other. I quicken my steps toward the exit door, and she follows me. How many steps have I taken? I do not know. How many more until I reach the exit? I do not know. But I hear the sound of his door opening, and the silence that falls over all other sounds. I know he is now standing at his room's door, rapidly sliding the beads of his prayer rosary over one another. I know his brows are furrowed in a tight knot. I want to turn back, to drive a soldier's spear into his heart and spit in his face when I hear his deep voice echo down the hallway: "Zubayda! Wait, I want to see you."

Haniya whispers, "The Caliph is standing behind us. He's calling for you. He surely needs something. For God's sake, please stop. Where are you going, my lady?"

I bite my lip and twist my turquoise ring around my finger. A tear escapes from the corner of my eye. I cannot hold it back. I walk toward the door. Waiting, in Harun's view, means only one thing: giving in to the heart. And I do not want to be part of his schemes again. I must stand firm in my words. A lifetime of devotion and compromise is enough. My lips move: "We are going to prison."

2

I look at the narrow, endless steps. It's as if two eyes are gleaming in the darkness at the bottom. A cool breeze rises from the shadows and brushes against my face. I want to walk toward the blackness, to reach the end of the stairs, the place my brother Fadhl always spoke of in hushed tones: "That's not a prison. It's a graveyard. A dreadful one. Over the years, many men have walked in there on their own, and none of them ever came back. That's why they call it Sandy Graveyard."

I wet my dry lips, take a deep breath, and tear my eyes away from the narrow stairs. Haniya is staring at me, her eyes filled with fear. "Should we go back, my lady?" she asks.

She asked so many questions on the way from the palace to the prison that I told her everything, everything that happened after she left, everything I had chosen.

"No. It's not time to leave. I have something to do here."

I take a step toward Muslim, who stands behind Haniya. He has directed all his attention to the surroundings.

"Do I still have enough standing to be alone in this prison for an hour?"

Muslim stops keeping watch and lowers his eyes to the ground. A shy smile touches his lips. "You will always be our lady."

"Don't flatter me. You know I don't have much time. If Harun finds out you've gone against his orders, you could be in danger."

He tightens his grip on the spear and lowers his voice.

"The prison is empty, so there's no assigned guard. One way or another, I'll stall the palace guards and the camel driver who's come to take you. None of us have forgotten your kindness. No one has ever stood by the servants the way you did. If there's any risk, I'll take it."

I let out a quiet breath of relief. There's nothing left of being a noblewoman, but I can still count on the loyalty of the palace guards.

The day I decided not to turn a blind eye to them, to the maids and their stories, I never imagined that kindness would one day come back to save me.

I give Muslim a faint smile and squeeze Haniya's hand. My eyes return to the darkness at the bottom of the stairs.

"Come with me."

Haniya starts walking. Muslim's eyes follow her.

If I see a yes in her eyes, I'll make sure, no matter what, that Fadhl and I arrange their wedding.

Muslim's love cannot be hidden. I tread softly on the narrow stairs. From the first step to the second, Fadhl's words ring in my ears: "Harun al-Rashid knows exactly what he's doing. He sent the Imam to the

Sandy Graveyard. Sandi ibn Shahak is the jailer there, and I'm sure his heart is made not of clay but of flint. His eyes are bloodshot, his head bald, and there is a red mark on his face the size of a coin. He says years ago, once, his heart burned for a prisoner, and in response to that foolish compassion, he branded his own face."

"Lady, I'm scared. What if the Caliph becomes angry?"

I squeeze Haniya's hand. Her fingertips are cold.

"I know Harun well. His anger flares suddenly and then quickly fades. These days he is calm. What could he want that he hasn't already done? Since the martyrdom of the Imam, I pray for death every moment."

Haniya murmurs something I can't quite hear. We go down, down, and further down. After a weak turn, the stairs end. I glance back at the path we came from. A small shaft of light is visible. The prison is built to be utterly dark.

"Stay right here, Haniya. Do not enter while I'm inside the prison. Sit on the stairs and keep watch. Muslim is at the top of the stairs, and I am inside the prison. There is no place for fear."

"But, Lady..."

Her dark eyes were trembling. I glance at her short, full figure and say, "Don't be afraid, girl. I should have come here sooner, back when Musa ibn Jafar was a prisoner in this darkness. But Harun wouldn't allow it. This time, I want to listen to my heart's call. Before leaving, Hababeh whispered in my ear: whenever you're troubled, listen to your heart and follow it. She said if your soul is restless, if your spirit finds no peace by any means, go to the Imam's prison. The Imam's prison isn't an ordinary prison. It is a place full of light and mystery. Haniya travelled from Medina to Baghdad chasing the call of her heart, searching for the scent and trace of the Imam. But I didn't dare come from the Palace of Eternity all the way to the gates of Kufa and see Sandi ibn Shahak's prison up close because of Harun's fear. You, who have travelled with Hababeh for so long, know his words better than I do. Do you remember his voice? Warm and light, it flew from his mouth and settled gently on the heart."

Tears pool in Haniya's eyes. She sits on the stairs and asks, "What really goes on inside that prison?"

"The walls and stones of that prison have held Musa ibn Jafar's loneliness for a long time. There is a storm raging inside me, Haniya. I'm going to go in and be alone for a while. I want to remember Hababeh's coming once more, his words and his leaving. I've been through hard days and made a difficult decision. There are no more secrets in my heart. But God knows the turmoil inside this chest will not quiet down. I keep thinking I am searching for something lost. You came and brought the news of Hababeh's passing. It struck me to come to this prison. Maybe here I can find a way to calm my broken heart."

Haniya nods silently. I press my hand against the wall and move forward. The prison's darkness swallows me whole. I see nothing; it is pitch black, as if black ink has been splattered across the walls. How could they have imprisoned the Imam in such a place? How could a heart made of stone endure the suffering of the Messenger's son? Why couldn't I do anything? Why couldn't I send the Imam to a better prison? A place where he could see the sunlight? How can you not be ashamed, Zubayda? How could you carry someone like Harun in your heart all these years? Shame on me for being alive, for still breathing. A lump tightens my throat. Slowly, with my hand on the wall, I move forward. A pleasant scent of jasmine drifts in. I take another step, but I fall face-first to the ground. Mud's wetness spreads over my face. My knees burn, my palms tingle. I painfully and silently lift my face from the ground. The saltiness of blood runs in my mouth. My pupils adjust to the dark. The edge of my skirt gets caught on a large stone. I struggle to free my skirt, a sharp pain stings my body, and I pull myself together. This is not Harun's palace, where maidens gather around me and flutter like butterflies - warm blood streaks down my chin. I wipe the fresh red blood with the edge of my sleeve and struggle to pull myself up from the ground. Squinting, I see in front of me a small cage-like room built with iron bars narrow, cramped, and terrifying. My knees tremble. I ignore the pain in my hand and move forward.

Fazel said, "Sandi's prison isn't very large. Why would it need to be? It's a slaughterhouse for the caliph's special guests, those he doesn't want to see peace, those he wants crushed under pressure. Harun only sends those there whose lives he intends to take."

The iron door of the barred cell opens with a howl-like screech. Longing and loneliness clutch at my heart. This damp, dark prison where the wind howls and no light pierces the brightness of day, these black stone walls, these thick iron bars, have long been my Imam's home.

I step forward, further in. Now I am inside the cage of bars where my Imam once breathed, where he stood in prayer, fell into prostration, and whispered his mystical prayers. Tears overcome me. The lump in my throat is not from a day or two's grief; it is the weight of years of yearning and denial. My sorrow is a thorn in my throat, a thorn that has always accompanied me through joy and pain. My sorrow is born of a dark love that has borne nothing but distance from the Prophet's children.

I lean my head against the wall, hoping my heart will find a crack in this prison, a crack toward the light. A drop of blood trickles from the corner of my lip onto the dirt. Harun's hands are stained with the blood of God's best servants.

For the first time, I allow my grief to break free. I want, just once, to weep for my Imam without fear, the Imam whose love and devotion I buried deep in my heart all my life, the innocent Imam murdered by Harun, the same Harun who was once dearer to me than life itself but whom I now loathe. A man whose rotten heart's stench had filled the city, and I realised it too late, on that cold, night, the night Hababeh came...

--- ◆ ---

I want to run. I want to race down this marble hallway and scream. What just happened? What suddenly changed? Just an hour ago, everything seemed fine, peaceful even. When Haniya brought word that Harun had called for me, I thought, as always, that he had grown lonely and missed me. I stood in front of the mirror, unwilling, slipped into my long black robe, put on my velvet slippers, and went to his chamber. But he wasn't alone.

Now that I've walked out of Harun's chamber, my cheeks burning and my heart fluttering like a trapped bird, I know deep down it's truly over between us. Tonight, Harun was a stranger. The man who used to call me Lady Zubayda, Lady, Mother of Amin, stood in front of a room full of men who once wouldn't have dared raise their eyes to me, and he shouted. Their smirks followed me as I walked away. I feel crushed, as if the crystal of my heart has fallen and shattered into a thousand pieces. I went to him with grace, but I left feeling broken, like I had crumbled to dust in his presence.

I should have spoken. I should have hurled every truth in my heart at his face. I should have stood tall before him. Something flutters in my chest. Heat rises from the floors, from the walls, and crashes down on me. One of the palace women walks past. I clench my teeth and keep walking, firm and steady. I just need to reach my room. There, I'll let the tears come. But not here.

"Lady, please wait." Haniya's voice stops me. I pause in the hallway. But before I can turn around, another voice calls out behind me. "Well, well, greetings to the Caliph's beloved lady. How are you, Zubayda? You didn't attend our gathering. I was worried you might be unwell."

One of the palace women is standing behind me. I force a smile onto my face. My lips stretch. When did I learn to fake a laugh like this?

"Hello, Salma dear. I'm not unwell, just a bit busy."

She's about to respond when I turn to Haniya and ask, "What is it?" She's out of breath, wiping sweat from her forehead, hands on her knees.

"Lady, there's an old woman here asking for you."

Salma cuts in before I can answer. "Another beggar, no doubt, holding out her bowl. Ever since you became mistress of this palace, the place is crawling with gypsies and peddlers."

"What's wrong with that, Salma dear? We're all God's servants, aren't we?"

Salma shrugs. I don't wait for her to reply and start walking toward my room. I don't have the strength to stand around.

"Lady..."

"What is it, Haniya? What do you want now?"

"You didn't answer me. What should I do with the old woman?"

"See what she needs. Give her water, food, a coin, and a cloak. Whatever she needs to leave in peace."

Haniya shifts from foot to foot.

"No, my lady. This old woman is different. There's something about the way she speaks... it touches the heart. Muslim says she's been sitting by the palace gate since dawn, hasn't moved an inch, and replies to the guards' harshness with nothing but sweetness. I went to see her myself. She's frail, bent over. She says she doesn't want anything, but she's only come to see you. That you're the reason she's here."

A sharp pulse throbs at my temples. The world begins to spin. On this endless night, when every moment has struck me like a hammer, now this old woman too? All these years, no one has ever come just to see me. They've all wanted something: a favour, a prayer, a dream granted. She's probably no different. "Haniya, I'm not feeling well. Speak to her yourself. Let her leave satisfied." "Oh dear, you're not feeling well? Alright, I'll go. But... Muslim says that around noon prayer, the old woman disappeared for a while. He went looking for her and saw her performing ablutions in a quiet corner." I wait for her to continue. She looks around, then leans in and whispers, "Muslim says she washes like the Rafidis[1]."

---

[1] Rāfiḍī (رافضي): A historical derogatory term used by some Sunni polemicists to refer to Shia Muslims, particularly those who "rejected" (rafadha) the political authority of the

Heat rushes to my cheeks. A Shia woman? So close to the palace? Just yesterday, by Harun's command, two Shia poets were beheaded along with their wives. If Harun finds out about her… waves of dread flood my chest.

"Has Muslim told anyone about her being a Rafidi?"

"No, my lady. He's your loyal servant. And he himself…"

"Say nothing more, Haniya."

Haniya nods. Harun was right to fear Imam Kadhim ﷺ. He was right not to let people speak with him. A man whose words could turn the palace guards and handmaidens into Shia; if he had lived and taken the throne, there would be nothing left of Harun al-Rashid's power and grandeur.

"Go, Haniya. Bring that old woman to the palace gate."

Haniya quickens her pace. Muslim is waiting at the end of the corridor, near the great brazier. She runs, and the flesh on her bones shakes with every step. She was just a seven-year-old girl when Harun gave her to me. Her dark eyes and round, full cheeks won me over instantly. I take my eyes off Haniya and glance around the hallway. I look at the white marble, the mirrorwork on the ceiling, the chandeliers and candles, the crystal and velvet drapes. Before the Imam's martyrdom, all of this seemed beautiful to me, like something from a dream. But ever since, the world has turned dark.

Harun's face and the fire in his eyes flood my thoughts. Over the years, I've often been hurt by what he's done, yet still held love for him in my

---

first caliphs and upheld the exclusive leadership of Imam 'Ali and his descendants. Over time, it became a general slur for the Shia community, though many Shia scholars later reclaimed the term as signifying rejection of falsehood and loyalty to the Ahl al-Bayt.

heart. All it took was to see him, and my knees would tremble, my legs give way. Love was the elixir that concealed all his cruelty. From my youth until now, as a middle-aged woman, all the days and hours have been filled with the sweetness of his voice whispering, "Zubayda," and I would laugh shyly, my cheeks flushing, and say, "My life for yours." He was a man, strong and unshakable, and I, with all my softness, had made his heart tremble.

When he saw me enter a gathering, proud and unshakable as always, his eyes would light up. His expression would soften, his lips curl into a smile. Everyone could tell something had shifted in him, that some of his power had melted away. They all knew Zubayda had arrived. That's why they came to me for the impossible. They were certain Zubayda could make the impossible happen. But after the Imam was arrested, after he ordered the son of Zahra ﷺ to be martyred… Grief grips my throat. My eyes fill with tears. I feel like I'm standing on the edge of collapse.

A knock at the hall door pulls me back. I push away my thoughts and look up. She's there, walking slowly behind Haniya. Her long grey robe trails along the floor. A few strands of white hair escape from beneath her black scarf. Her face is creased and worn, and her sagging cheeks remind me of a crushed pomegranate. She comes closer. The years have dusted her honey-coloured eyes, but they remain beautiful.

Haniya steps to my side. The old woman fixes her gaze on me. Then, once, twice, three times, she looks me up and down. Her lips begin to move.

"Praise to the great and protecting God, that my eyes have been blessed to behold the beauty of Zubayda bint Jafar."

I step forward.

"You wanted to see me? What's your name?"

"I am Hababeh al-Walbiya, my daughter. I've longed to see your face, to breathe in your scent. I've been waiting since morning for this. I was afraid I might have to leave Baghdad before meeting you."

I raise an eyebrow. My ears are used to hearing things like, "I am poor, helpless, alone. I've come hoping for a crust of bread, a coin, a robe..."

"What is your business? Where are you going? What brought you to Baghdad?"

She smiles, scratches a mole near her lips with her trembling hand, and says, "My business is love. My heart is all I own. I came from Medina, hoping to breathe in the same air as a noble and beloved man. I stayed in Baghdad for a while, praying for a chance to see his face. But it didn't happen. My longing and devotion weren't enough to overcome your caliph's power and cruelty. I learned too late that he was here in Baghdad. Woe to me, he was imprisoned, and I was free. Still, I take comfort knowing I breathed the same air he did, that I slept beneath the same sky as he did in this city. That alone is enough for me. There was nothing I could do but pack my things and struggle for one brief moment in his presence."

Her words sound like no one else's. The corner of my eye twitches, and I blink several times. Her lips, as thin as thread, move, and a sound escapes that sends a chill down my spine. I know who she's talking about. I know exactly what she means. But I don't want to believe it. Maybe it's all some trick. Or maybe it's just a dream.

"What are you saying, old woman? Who are you talking about?"

She comes closer, leaning hard on her cane. With a soft cough, she answers, "Our Imam. Musa ibn Jafar ﷺ."

I bite my lip. How dare she speak so boldly? Does she not know that even uttering the name of Zahra's descendants in Harun al-Rashid's palace could cost her life?

"That's enough. Say your business and go. I don't have time to listen to your words."

Her smile fades, but her eyes still shine. She tucks a few loose strands of hair back under her scarf.

"Very well. It's nothing really, Lady Zubayda. I came to speak a secret that's lived in my heart... I've been searching for you for a long time. You were hard to find. All I had was a name, Zubayda bint Jafar. I didn't know how to reach you. I came to Baghdad longing to see the child of Zahra, but your name found its way to me instead. A saying of Imam Sadiq ﷺ stirred in my memory. I asked the people of the city, and I became sure you were the one, the unseen companion. I made a vow to myself that before I left, I would meet you. Perhaps I wouldn't get another chance. But if you wish it, I'll go now."

"What secret? What hadith? I don't understand what you're saying. Wouldn't it be better to stop speaking in riddles?"

The old woman smiles and takes my hand. Her hands are warm. I like their warmth.

"Dear, my secret is mine to keep... I can't sum it up in a single word. It's a long story. But if you want to hear it..."

A secret. So she, too, carries one, just like me? When she first arrived, she looked like any other old woman. But now, something in her words has stirred me deep inside. I can feel the weight of the other women's stares, fixed on her, on her faded clothes and the brown patched shoes on her feet.

"How am I supposed to trust you?"

"My daughter, light of my eyes... are you truly afraid of an old, hunched woman with nothing in her hands? I heard there are seven doors between here and Harun's chambers, all guarded, but you, beloved of the poor and famed for your courage, shouldn't let fear take root in your heart. Rest assured. Among all these maids and guards, I will not make a single false move. I carry no weapon, no poison. I have brought no protector and no companion. God alone is my witness and my strength."

I play with my ring. The weight of this night is like a punishment that keeps returning. It never ends. I breathe deeply. The air smells of frankincense and rue. I believe in signs, in the way not even a leaf falls from the palace trees without permission. And now, as Harun's bitter cries echo through the halls, this hunched old woman arrives. I have to cling to this sign. I don't understand why she's here, but I feel like I know her, her gaze, her scent, the gleam in her eyes. I want to invite her into my room, but she reaches for the shawl wrapped around her waist. I fall silent and watch her trembling hand.

"You're right, Lady Zubayda. I need to earn your trust. You are right, dear one. Let me show you something to put your mind at ease."

I narrow my eyes as the old woman pulls out a white cloth. A flower is stitched on it in green thread. She places the fabric in my hand.

"I never imagined I would bring this heavenly gift out here in Shaddad's paradise under Harun al-Rashid. I'm sure it's fate. Open it. I don't have much time."

Without saying a word, I unwrap the cloth. Inside, a small stone lies, black and smooth.

"Turn the stone over, my dear."

Haniya stretches her neck to see the stone. I don't know why, but my hand trembles. I glance at the old woman. She smiles and nods. I hold the stone between my fingers, my eyes filling with tears. On the hard black stone, there is a ring seal. I recognise this seal. It belongs to Imam Musa al-Kazim ﷺ.

I want to hug the old woman and kiss her hands, but Haniya tugs at my sleeve and whispers, "Lady, the caliph's minister is coming your way."

I gather my trembling chin with effort and nod. The stone is hidden in my palm as I place my hand behind Hababeh's back. "Go to my room with Haniya and wait for me."

The old woman looks at me with hesitation, coughing softly and biting her lip. Haniya shows her the way, and though the old woman's eyes stay fixed on me, she picks up her pace as she heads toward the room.

I turn toward the minister. Harun must have sent a message.

Voices of a veiled age

Voices of a veiled age

3

Hababeh is sitting on the bed, watching me. I close the door and lean against it. The stone engraved with the Imam's seal is clenched in my fist. Haniya steps forward.

"My lady! Are you feeling unwell? Oh, heavens! Let me bring you a glass of sherbet," she says."

I want to say I'm fine, that there's nothing wrong, but she doesn't wait for an answer. My throat is dry, parched like a desert untouched by rain. Hababeh rises and takes my hand. She leads me to the bed and gently says, "These joined eyebrows, that long face, your tall, graceful frame, it all makes you look like a mountain, solid and unshakable. But behind your eyelids, there's something that betrays you, something that screams: even a mountain can have a heart as fragile as a flower. Why are you fighting so hard? What did that man say to you in the hallway that left you so shaken?"

The minister's wheat-colored face, with its sparse but long beard, flashes before my eyes. He stood in front of me, raised his voice to the ceiling, and said, "The Commander of the Faithful has ordered you to appear before him at once and answer the questions you left unanswered tonight. You know he cannot stand being kept waiting."

I shouted louder than he did: "My answer was ready. It was your Caliph who wouldn't let me speak. I've been preparing to answer that question for a long time."

"My daughter, there's no colour in your face. From the moment I saw you, your eyes have looked heavy with sadness. They spill their sorrow into the heart of anyone who meets them. What is it, mother? What's hiding behind those eyes?"

For the first time, someone had truly seen it, the bitterness in my gaze, the weight of grief piling up inside me. For years, I wasn't myself. For years, I played a part. Hiding who you are, pretending to be someone you're not, it wears you down. With every passing day, every night that turns into morning, you lose a piece of yourself. And each time you look in the mirror, you see a stranger. Someone who looks like you, but only her lips are smiling. It's a deep kind of pain when your eyes have lost their light.

I hadn't been myself for years, since the day I wanted to run outside and play with the children in the courtyard, to sit in the dirt and come home tired at dusk, but I wasn't allowed. Being a descendant of the Abbasids wasn't a small thing. When I rode through the city in a Howdah, I would stare at the children and they would stare back. I envied their freedom and they envied my life.

As I grew older, all I wanted was to stay up all night listening to my mother's stories, to hear about the hard days she had survived, the days of her servitude. But I couldn't. I had to go to bed early, spend my days with a handmaiden, and pretend my mother hadn't once been a slave, carrying a world of pain and poverty.

When I married Harun, I wanted to be a woman in love, a woman who lived by her heart. But that wasn't possible. Being the lady of the palace took strategy, a certain kind of cleverness. In private, I was Harun's beloved. In public gatherings, I was Zubayda, the strong and determined noblewoman.

All my life, I longed to walk among the poor, to sit with them, to listen to their stories. But the circumstances demanded otherwise. I had to hear their cries from the height of a howdah, from behind a curtain, and send them gifts instead.

After Amin was born, I wanted nothing more than to be a mother with a quiet mind, to give my son all of myself. But half my attention had to remain with the state, making sure Harun did not become a puppet in the hands of the Barmakids, reminding him that being Caliph wasn't just about power and wine.

I understood politics. Sitting through my grandfather's lessons had taught me how to view the kingdom's affairs. But inside me lived a woman full of hope, full of noise, who wanted to live freely and break away from all the glitter. But she couldn't. Her love for Harun and life in the palace had bound her hands and feet.

Each day that passed, I let go of a part of Zubayda and rebuilt her again. But my belief never changed. My heart belonged to Harun, but my faith was with the descendants of Ali ﷺ. Two loves in one heart. To hold both, I had to wear a mask at all times. And in time, that mask became part of me.

I saw the injustices my husband committed. I understood the Imam's loneliness. But I had no right to speak. I knew well that Harun was mine, a kind and loving husband, as long as I never moved a finger in defence of the children of Zahra.

So I hid my beliefs and only cried at night in private for my shattered heart. But after the Imam was arrested, when I fell at Harun's feet begging to see my Imam just once, and he sneered, when I pleaded for a warm morsel of food to be sent to the Imam, he withheld even dry bread, and when the news of the Imam's martyrdom reached me, all my love for Harun turned into hatred. Now a lifetime of silence, a lifetime of fear, a lifetime of playing a role has piled up inside me, and I can no longer bear to swallow my pain and stay silent.

Hababeh squeezes my hands. I come back to myself, push away my thoughts, and she looks at me with a smile as if she's stitched it onto her lips.

"Speak to me, my dear."

I twist my ring and stare at its beautiful turquoise. A heavy lump tightens my throat. A single tear falls from my eye. I lift my hand and hold the stone toward her.

"Why have you come all this way? Where did you get this stone, old woman?"

Hababeh gathers my tears with her fingertips, takes the stone from my hand, and kisses it.

"Will you sit down? Sit down and be still? I'm not here to harm you, daughter."

I sit, lean against the pillow, and watch her. She sits beside me. The sweet scent of her clothes fills my senses.

She gazes at the stone and says, "This stone has been the greatest treasure of my life for years. My Imam blessed it for me, with his holy hands."

I lower my voice and ask, "Did you see Musa ibn Jafar in person?"

She wraps the stone in a white embroidered cloth. Then she tucks it into her sash.

"Yes. I have seen him, as well as the six Imams ﷺ before him. At dawn, when the morning breaks, I set out with the caravan for Medina to see Ali ibn Musa al-Ridha ﷺ and ask him to stamp this stone. This is my mission."

Questions swirl in my mind. Is it possible for a woman her age to have truly known Imam Ali ﷺ all the way to Musa ibn Jafar ﷺ? How many days and nights have these eyes seen? This stone, this seal... what mission?

"What is the story of this stone?"

She takes her eyes off me and fixes her gaze on the vase full of flowers on the shelf. It's as if she's staring into the farthest edge of the world.

"Sit down, and I'll tell you. This stone has a strange story. Many years ago, just after the Prophet of God passed away, the Muslims were burning with grief and longing for him. Ali was standing on the pulpit delivering a sermon. I was there at that gathering. Some people were whispering about the caliphate during Ali's speech. We all remembered the event of Ghadir, but some wanted to forget it. Ali's words reached the topic of Imamate after prophethood. To silence the murmurs in the assembly, I asked, 'O Ali, what is the sign of Imamate?' The Imam pointed to a corner of the mosque. He showed me this small stone and asked me to put it in his hand. Amid the silence of the crowd, I took the stone and went to him. Ali pressed his ring onto the stone. The hard, unyielding rock softened like wax in his hands, and the mark of the ring sank into its heart. He held the stone out to me and said to the crowd, "Whoever can leave a seal on this stone is the rightful Imam." From that day on, I knew what I had to do. With the appointment of each of Ali and Fatima's sons as Imam, I would go to him and deliver the stone. To be honest, the first time I stood before Imam Hasan ﷺ, I didn't know how to explain the story of the stone. I hesitated, caught between speaking and staying silent. Then he looked at me and gave a sign. I stepped forward, still unsure, and he said, "Hababeh, come here and give me the stone." That's when I understood this stone was a lasting sign, a mark to prove the truth of Ali's family.

After Imam Hasan ﷺ, I went to five more Imams. There was never any need to speak. Each time, I placed the stone in their hands, and the seal of Imamate would appear within it…Tomorrow morning, I'll leave with the caravan for Medina. It's time to take the stone to Ali ibn Musa al-Ridha ﷺ. Now tell me about yourself… Did you ever meet Imam Kadhim ﷺ?"

I can't take my eyes off the old woman before me, white-haired, hunched, like someone out of a story.

Voices of a veiled age

She feels like a dandelion drifting in with good news. Her words carry the scent of truth. When she speaks of Ali, her gaze clears, and the wrinkles around her eyes fade.

Her pupils shine, and her words sink deep into the heart. My heart believes her. I want to speak to her. This stone alone is enough to make me trust her. I'm certain that someone who loves the descendants of Ali ﷺ this deeply can be a patient listener, a trusted soul. God has sent her to me. I wet my lips, wrap my arms around my knees, and whisper: "Everyone thinks I'm drowning in happiness, the women in the palace glare at me with envy in their eyes. To them, I'm the luckiest woman alive, the favourite of Harun al-Rashid. But inside me, there's a storm only God knows about. When I see the palace women and hear their wishes, I sometimes think, if only I could live like them. If only my biggest worry was choosing a gold-threaded dress or receiving royal jewels as gifts. If only I could spend my days at women's gatherings, carefree, and laugh beside my husband at the evening feasts. But I'm not like them. I haven't been for years. I've been at war with myself for a long time. Tonight, just before you arrived, Harun called me to his room and questioned me. He asked what I believed in, what I truly stood for. He asked if I believed in the descendants of Ali. He shouted and kept pressing me with questions. I don't know who told him. I'm not afraid that he found out. Honestly, when I think about the consequences of my choice and the punishment that may come, I do feel some fear. But I'm certain of one thing. I want to stand up to Harun. Tonight, I wanted to shout it in front of everyone. I wanted to say, "I am a follower of the descendants of Ali." But he didn't let me speak. It felt like he already knew my answer and just wanted to give me one last chance to take it back. But I won't take it back. Whatever is going to happen, let it happen. Nothing can be worse than the death of my Imam. Harun had him killed, and I did nothing. I couldn't do anything. He says he loves me, but he never once let me visit my Imam. For years, I longed to see him. When Harun brought him to Baghdad, my heart overflowed with hope. Not because he was imprisoned. That broke my heart. But because I thought I might finally see him. But that meeting never really happened. Just once, and even then, only from a distance."

There's a quiet knock at the door. Haniya comes in, carrying a tray with a jug of saffron syrup. She pours a glass and hands it to me, then fills another for Hababeh.

"You look better. Has the colour come back to your cheeks?"

Her worry feels kind to me. I nod.

"Yes. Go on now and see to dinner. I have a special guest tonight."

Haniyah glances at Hababeh, her lips moving softly. "Yes, ma'am." Then she slips out of the room.

Those who love the descendants of Ali are always close to my heart. But this old woman feels even dearer than the rest. I drink the syrup in one long breath.

Henna starts to speak: "Zubayda, Zubayda..."

The cup in Hababeh's hand goes still. She lifts her head, surprised, eyes searching for the voice. I smile.

"She's a lovely bird."

"My companion. She listens, but says nothing."

"What's her name?"

"Henna. Lady Henna."

Hababeh smiles. "When you smile, that dimple in your cheek makes you even more beautiful."

I look down. Harun once said he loved that dimple. He used to tell me he buried his sorrows in it. But he lied.

"You were saying, my daughter. Tell me, where did you see our Imam? What was his condition?"

I like this word, our Imam. For the first time, I feel I am not a stranger or alone. I lace my fingers together and stretch my numb leg on the bed. "When Harun brought the Imam to Baghdad, he handed him over to Fadhl. He is my brother."

"Does your brother know the secret of your heart?"

"No. I have never said that I have affection for the children of Lady Zahra. Fadhl hasn't either. But I knew he did not want to torture the Imam. The same night I heard that the Imam had been moved to Fadhl's prison, I went to his house. All I asked was that he not be harsh with the Imam. Fadhl kept chewing his moustache and said the presence of the Imam had placed him in a state of torment, one side of which was heaven and the other side hell. He was afraid of Harun. He had a right to be. He had often seen how the fire of Harun's anger destroyed people's lives."

Hababeh's cough cuts off my words. I look at her. Since I saw her, she has not stopped coughing. It calms for a moment and then returns. She drinks some syrup and nods for me to go on. I fill my chest with the scent of frankincense in the room.

"That day, when I saw Fadhl still hesitating, I told him not to worry about Harun. I said, whatever happens, I would not let my brother, the uncle of Amin, the heir to the caliphate, be harmed. Somehow, he agreed. The Imam stayed in a small house next to Fadhl's palace, a house with a small door and tall walls. Guards with spears surrounded the house. Every day, I found some excuse to go to Fadhl's residence. As soon as I got close to the house, a sweet fragrance would fill me. I felt as if peace had been sprinkled over that place. Do you understand what I mean?"

Hababeh nods.

"I understand. If that peace wasn't heavenly, I would never have come all the way from Medina to Baghdad like a child searching for her mother."

Regret wells up inside me. She came all this way for her Imam, and I... I let out a weary sigh and continue: "One evening at sunset, tired and low like every other day, I went to Fadl's house. I remember it well. On the way, a widow stopped me and broke into sobs. She spoke of her sick husband and her hungry children. She said she herself was being crushed under the weight of life. Women like her are not in short supply in this city. Baghdad, for all its beauty and splendour, is full of poor people who can't afford bread. But at that time, Harun was at the height of his pleasures while the people lived in hardship and poverty. I thought to myself that something had to be done."

Hababeh rests her hand under her chin. "Harun should be proud to have a wife like you. God sent you to this city to help its people. Since I've been in Baghdad, I've heard a lot about your generosity."

My generosity does nothing to ease the suffering of the Shia in this city. How many of Ali's followers have I saved from Harun's sword until now? I shake my head and ignore Hababeh's praise.

Voices of a veiled age

"That day, when Fadhl saw my sadness and grief, he gestured toward the rooftop and asked, 'Would you like to go up there to see the beauty of Baghdad better? Seeing Al-Khuld Palace and the Palace of Yahya al-Barmaki, which grows more splendid every day, from above is a different kind of pleasure.'" I followed him without a word. We climbed the stairs together and stepped out onto the rooftop. I was about to complain about Harun and talk about the poor woman, but suddenly I realised what was really happening. I finally understood Fadl's intention. My mouth went dry, and my heart felt like it was going to burst out of my chest. I had asked Fadhl many times to take me to meet the Imam, but he had always refused. A strange excitement ran through every fibre of my being. My eyes smiled, and a voice raced through my mind, "My Imam... my Imam..." Fadhl was standing at the edge of the rooftop, resting his weight against the short wall and staring down. I stood behind his large frame and sensed the guard's fixed gaze. Fadhl whispered, "Look down. See inside the room." I nearly fainted. I felt life draining from my fingertips. I was burning up; my face felt like it was on fire. Tears danced in my eyes, and I had no chance to blink. Musa ibn Ja'far ﷺ was praying right before my eyes. The rooftop of Fadhl's palace overlooked the prison, or rather a small room within a narrow courtyard with tall, oppressive walls. The door to the room in the courtyard was open, and the Imam was prostrating on a small mat. After a while, darkness spread across the sky. But there was no lantern. When I protested to my brother about the Imam having no light, he said, "Harun has forbidden the Imam to have any light." My heart bled. Even now, when I think of the darkness of that room and the Imam's loneliness, my whole body burns, and I wish I could gouge out Harun's eyes. That half-seen moment was the only time I saw my Imam.

Hababeh wipes her tears with the corner of her scarf. "Harun thought that if he denied the Imam a lantern, it would make things hard for him. I wish he knew that if the Imam wished, he could command the sun and the moon themselves. Tell me, how could you ever love a man like him?"

"There was a time when Harun was my very life. Without him, I wanted no part of this world. But now, sitting here before you, I thirst for his blood. I wish him the worst fate imaginable. If I could, I would tear out his throat with my own teeth. My love for him grew slowly over the years, but my hatred, after my Imam was martyred, flared so fiercely that no affection remained in me. Love may come little by little, but hatred shows itself all at once."

"How did you change so much?"

"When I saw the injustice done to my Imam, the world went dark before my eyes. I had always believed I could do something to save the children of Zahra. All these years, I thought I could protect my Imam through Harun's affection for me. But I could do nothing. Hababeh, what is a piece of bread that even Harun would not place before the Imam? How can I love a man with the nature of a wolf? A man whose lust for power and wealth has blinded him."

Hababeh furrows her brows. "My girl, your love was never truly love. It was born of instinct. True love must be a path to flight, not a road that leaves you grounded."

"How can you call the love that took root in me at seventeen legitimate?"

Voices of a veiled age

Hababeh's frown softens, she smiles again, shakes her head, and says, "When I asked around in the streets about your name and conduct to make sure you were truly Zubayda bint Jafar, I heard so much about your royal wedding. They say it was unlike anything ever seen before."

Hearing her words, for a moment, I am seventeen again, a young bride with a thousand dreams. What can I say about that magical night, a night whose every moment is still vivid before my eyes, a night that still brings color to my cheeks when I think of it. My wedding dress had a long train with pearls sewn along it. Around the neckline, on the shoulders, across the chest, and at the cuffs, it glittered with flawless diamonds and dazzling peridots. Harun wanted me to be the jewel among all the women of the palace, those who had come and those who would go after.

Hababeh is right; the description of our wedding is still on people's lips. Baghdad has never seen a ceremony as magnificent as that night. The corridors of Al-Khuld Palace gleamed with light. Everywhere I looked, there was brightness, colour, and beauty. Stunning chandeliers hung in every corner. Guests held cups filled with gold and silver. There was so much sherbet, sweets, ruby-red grapes, and other fruits that no one even reached for them anymore.

I stare at my hands, twist my ring around my finger, and murmur, "The night of my wedding was the most magical night of my life. It felt as if pearls were raining down on me. Harun poured handfuls of them over my head. I laughed, my heart racing, melting under his gaze. He had set up a feast like no other, giving the people of the city food, cloth, and jewels. Before the wedding, when I first heard whispers about this great banquet, I sent him a message asking that the Banu Hashim receive more than anyone else. He agreed without a word. How naïve I was to think his generosity would last forever!"

"Dear soul, kind Zubayda! No, you can't hold two loves in one heart."

I nod and draw my feet in. "You've come to the palace to see me. You spoke of Imam Sadiq's ﷺ words, of a hidden secret. I'm waiting."

"I have much to say, Zubayda. There are things in this heart you need to hear."

"Tonight, I'm giving you all my time. Talking with you, I think, will ease my sorrows and bring peace to my heart."

Hababeh shifts on the bed, coughs softly, presses her left knee, and smiles: "Since we're speaking of love, listen while I tell you the first story. To understand it all, you'll have to stay with me until dawn and hear the tales of women, each with her own strange fate. These stories are part of the secret you want to know. The first is about a woman named Sumaya, a woman even more in love than you. Are you ready to hear it?"

I nod my head. I listen with all my heart. Hababeh looks steadily at the Quran resting on the shelf, her lips moving softly.

— ◆ —

"Sumaya is worlds different from you. You are a lady of the palace, but she was a servant. The servant of Abi Hudhayfah, the chief of the Banu Makhzum tribe. She worked quietly, ate little, slept little, and no one ever heard her voice raised in protest. But then something happened that revealed Sumaya's true spirit. It was only then that everyone realised who she really was."

"One day, a young man arrived at the Banu Makhzum tribe, who turned Sumaya's life upside down. The young man was from Yemen and had come to Mecca in search of his younger brother. Yemen was suffering through a drought. When he lost hope of finding his brother, he decided to stay in Mecca. For this reason, he allied with the Banu Makhzum."

I rest my hand under my chin and stare at her mouth, while she gently rubs her knees and continues, "The young man from Yemen was tall and strong. Everyone liked him, from Abi Hudhayfah himself to the girls and servants of the tribe. Sumaya liked him too. But reaching that young man was an impossible dream. She thought, how could the servant of Abi Hudhayfah compare to a free and strong man? But fate had another plan for her and the young man. One day, Sumaya was baking bread when her thoughts turned to the young man from Yemen, and Abi Hudhayfah called for her. A wave of anxiety gripped Sumaya's heart. Abi Hudhayfah did not mingle with the servants. With fear, she entered Abi Hudhayfah's tent. Without any introduction, he raised his firm voice and said, 'I had decided to marry you to the young man from Yemen. There is no doubt about your goodness, beauty, and grace. You have grown up under my protection, and I have seen your modesty and chastity with my own eyes. But Walid also wants you. Your delicate face has captured his heart. You know he lacks nothing in wealth, and his influence is great… but my heart does not consent to this union. I prefer you to be with the young man from Yemen. On the other hand, saying no to Walid will anger him. Until now, no one has ever refused him. I have made my decision…' Sumaya didn't know whether to be happy or upset. She saw herself just a few steps away from union, but Walid was a fierce rival. Sometimes, no matter what you do, the affection of one person just never settles in your heart. Walid's affection never settled in

Sumaya's heart. She hated his long, hooked nose and gaunt face, and his thick, always-greasy hair made her blood boil. Every time Abi Hudhayfah's servants gathered, Walid's name came up. After all, he was wealthy, and alongside his greed for wealth, his hunger to possess women burned fiercely within him. Whether free or servant, the eldest daughter of the tribe or a slave-born, it made no difference to him. If Walid set his eyes on a woman, he chose her for marriage. Walid's wealth enchanted the other servants, but Sumaya feared him. To her, Walid looked evil. Everyone knew that by that day, he had buried three newborn daughters alive and had beaten one of his wives to death, burying her under the ground. Sumaya didn't want to live her whole life haunted by the fear of bearing daughters, only to have Walid one day give his own daughter to the desert and proudly speak of burying her alive. Then come upon her body with blows, lashes, and bruises."

I bite my lip and interrupt Hababeh, "Burying a newborn alive takes a heart as dark as night. The struggling and pleading of a woman as her baby is slowly pushed toward death is horrifying."

Hababeh raises her eyebrow, "Have you seen such a thing with your own eyes? That was an old Arab custom, one that ended with the coming of our Prophet ﷺ."

Abbasah's image is vivid before my eyes; her hands dancing, her cries echoing. That day she wore a beautiful purple dress. I take a deep breath and push Abbasah's image aside. "It doesn't matter, Hababeh. Don't lose your train of thought. Tell me, didn't Sumaya protest? Didn't she say her heart belonged to the young man from Yemen?"

Hababeh looks at me, her eyes calming my soul.

Voices of a veiled age

"All right, I won't ask. No, my daughter, there was nothing Sumaya could do. She was a servant; she had to obey whatever her master commanded, just like the servants who serve you and Harun in the palace. But God looked after Sumaya and her pure heart. Abi Hudhayfah became the means to save her. He set up a shooting contest between Walid and the young man from Yemen.

That day, the sun beat down on the desert as the competition between Walid and the Yemeni began. Sumaya watched from afar. First, Walid took his bow. When the arrow settled on the string, Sumaya's heart suddenly sank. Abi Hudhayfah nodded to a slave who was standing on a height holding two birds. The slave lifted the bird. Sumaya felt as if her entire future were laid out before her, and that her happiness and misery depended on that one arrow. At Abi Hudhayfah's signal, the servant ran toward the hill and, with a shout, sent the birds flying into the sky. The competition was the young Yemeni's only chance to prove his worth. After all, Walid was from the tribe and knew everyone, while the young stranger was alone. Walid was wealthy, and with half his fortune, he could buy dozens of women like Sumaya as slaves. Most importantly, Walid knew how to talk and draw people's attention, but the young Yemeni was not good with words. When the other slave girls heard about what had happened, they scolded Sumaya. They said Walid was superior in every way. But the heart plays by no rules of logic. Sumaya did not want Walid. The contest began, and the two birds wheeled through the sky. Walid poured all his strength into his hands and let his arrow fly. The bird flapped and fell to the ground. The sound of Walid's laughter made Sumaya's back tremble."

I see myself in the desert, a spectator beside Sumaya.

"Did the arrow hit the bird? Tell me, did Walid win? Poor Sumaya!" Hababeh takes a sip of sherbet, coughs, and goes on, "Listen, my dear! You're so impatient! The arrow had struck the bird, but the young Yemeni could still win. Walid's boasts did not shake him. He drew the bowstring all the way back, and large, wild beads of sweat ran from his forehead to his chin. The bird rose higher into the wide sky. The young man gathered all his focus and released the arrow. Sumaya's gaze followed it up to the roof of the sky. The arrow struck the bird's heart, and a few seconds later, the bird fell to the ground. Walid ground his teeth and moved to grab the young man's collar, but Abi Hudhayfah's voice rang out. 'Stop, Walid! I'll decide the outcome myself, and everyone will have to follow it.' At Abi Hudhayfah's signal, the servant ran toward the birds. He first picked up Walid's bird and held it in his right hand. Then he lifted the young Yemeni's bird with his left hand and stepped forward. Sumaya caught the young man's sidelong glance. She blushed, redder than before. The sun's heat burned her face, and the heat of the young man's gaze burned her inside. Walid wasn't looking at her. To him, Sumaya was prey, like the wounded bird in the servant's hand. The servant placed the birds before Abu Hudhayfah and said, 'This... this bird is still alive. It's breathing, its wings are moving. The arrow hurt its wing, but it has life. But this one, this bird the young Yemeni hunted, is like a lifeless stone. The arrow split its chest.' Walid shouted, growled, and sprang at the servant. Walid said the wager had been on striking, not killing, so there was no true victory in the contest."

I brush away a fly circling my head. Since childhood, whenever anxiety took hold of me, I would bite my lip. Then my grandfather would notice and say, "You've picked your lips again, Zubayda dear!" I release my lip.

"So, what happened in the end? Was there another match?" When I put myself in Sumaya's place, my heart fills with dread."

Hababeh laughs, "Don't worry. Sumaya was a slave with no one, but she had God. That day, Abu Hudhayfah ended the quarrel. He said the point of the contest was to test marksmanship, and Walid had not truly won. So the winner was the young Yemeni. Sumaya didn't know what to do with her joy, but Walid burned like a blazing furnace and shouted, 'Fine, I lost. But by al-Lat and al-'Uzza, I have plans for your misery. Wait for me, Sumaya bint Khayyat!' The next day, when Abu Hudhayfah placed Sumaya's hand in Yasir's, he declared that she was no longer a slave. In honour of her marriage to the young Yemeni, he had granted her freedom. That freedom completed Sumaya's happiness, but the dark shadow of Walid did not lift from her life."

I see Sumaya with her not-so-fair skin, small eyes, and fleshy nose sitting across from me, looking at me. Hababeh is silent. I twist my turquoise ring and ask, "What happened? Did Walid finish Yasir off and take Sumaya for himself? Yes? If I were Sumaya, I'd end Walid in his sleep."

Hababeh looks at me in surprise and removes her headscarf. Her silver hair is short and thin. Without the headscarf, the wrinkles under her chin stand out more. She sets the scarf beside her and tucks a few strands of hair behind her ear.

"From an intelligent and prudent woman like you, I wouldn't expect such a thing. No, Walid wanted to make Sumaya's life bitter, little by little. Only three days had passed since their wedding when Yasir came home, upset and gloomy. He said he had been dismissed from the trading house where he worked. When Sumaya heard this, she weakened. She poured the cooked chickpeas into a bowl and set them on the table with dry bread and a jug of yogurt drink. Something gripped her heart, something like loneliness and exile. Still, Yasir was hopeful. He said that in the morning he'd go looking for a new job, that he'd even put aside a little money for hard times. But Sumaya knew this was Walid's doing. Because of his great wealth, everyone feared Walid. On top of that, the elders of Mecca protected him. The sorrow of that night returned to Sumaya's heart. She thought to herself, 'They say I am free, yet the mark of a slave is forever stamped on my forehead. Their cruelty has no end. Walid is like a wounded snake. His oppression and that of men like him is backed by the elders of Mecca. A black woman, a slave, a stranger like me has no place in their circle.' Zubayda! She knew no fear of poverty. She had spent her whole life serving as a slave in the Banu Makhzum tribe and every night had found a morsel to eat. She had learned to be content with the smallest things. Just having a shelter, and after all these years, a man like Yasir to support her that was worth the world. But her heart was heavy. In Mecca, the rich grew stronger day by day, while the rest struggled in the pit of poverty and misery. Power belonged to the tribes. They spilled blood, buried girls alive, enslaved black men and women, set animals against humans for entertainment, and crushed anyone who opposed their will. Some by killing, others by exile, and others like them through suffering. Sumaya and Yasir endured hard times, but a year later, the hardest night of their lives came."

I take a deep breath. To have no one on your side, to feel like a stranger among people, to have no one understand or support you is terrifying. Again, the corner of my eye twitches, over and over.

"Which night, Hababeh? What happened?"

Voices of a veiled age

Hababeh touches her head and coughs, dry coughs, one after another.

"Take a sip of water."

I take her hand gently.

"Do you want to rest?"

She kisses my cheek, and my heart tightens.

"We don't have time, my dear. We don't have time! I have to leave early in the morning, and I promised to share my secret with you before I go. These stories have to end tonight."

I nod.

"Zubayda, you have a child, don't you?"

I thought of Amin, the boy who looks so much like Harun.

"I have a son. His name is Amin."

"Do you remember the night he was born?"

When Amin was born, the world changed colours. Harun could not stop saying 'Um Amin.' He was constantly around me, holding Amin in his arms, whispering words of love into my ear, and sometimes singing softly. 'Harun, my crown, the light of Zubayda's eyes, what if you stopped tormenting the children of the Messenger of God? Their sighs will catch up with us; they will catch up with Amin. Let them live in peace, free from torture, prison, and fear. For the sake of our son's birth, lay down your arms against them. You know they have the right; they are the rightful successors of the Messenger.' The moment I said those words, Harun's face went pale. His pupils widened, and his brows furrowed tightly. Until that day, I had never seen him bare his teeth at me. He said nothing. He simply placed Amin in my arms and walked away. He didn't come the next day, nor the day after. On the third day, Haniyah brought news that Harun had given his heart to one of Yahya's slave girls. She said he visited her many times a day and sent her precious gifts. Since Harun had taken the throne, Yahya al-Barmaki was constantly at the palace, ready to obey Harun's every command, until finally Harun made him his minister. That day when I heard the news from Haniya, the sorrow of the world overflowed in my heart, and I gasped like a fish out of water. I was wide open, helpless. I was simple; I loved him because I still didn't believe in the demon inside him. In my naive imagination, I wanted to bring him back to me, back to life. My feminine pride wouldn't let me go to him or send anyone after him. So, I gathered all the poets and scholars of the palace. They all came. I asked them to compose poems celebrating loyalty and condemning betrayal, songs of longing and love. They wrote their verses, and the palace girls memorised them. Then I arranged for the girls to go to Harun and recite the poems to him. My plan worked. A few hours after the girls left, Harun came to me. The anger was gone. He was the same Harun I once knew. He slipped this turquoise ring onto my finger and breathed in Amin's scent. He said nothing about Yahya's slave girl, only said, 'My heart felt a strange ache, a longing.' A few days later, when Haniyah reported that Harun no longer visited Yahya's slave girl, I was overjoyed. Damn me for not standing up then to defend the children of the Messenger of God, for not confronting him."

I push those thoughts aside and look at Hababeh, who waits patiently. I say, "Yes, that night was unlike any other. The women of the palace came to help me. The best wet nurses were by my side."

Hababeh nods.

"Almost every woman has someone to help them at that moment. But that night, Sumaya was alone. The room still smelled of sleep when her cries pierced the sky. She clawed at the ground, screaming. Yasir heard his wife's loud voice for the first time and woke with a start. Large beads of sweat had formed on Sumaya's forehead. She writhed in pain and shouted, 'Yasir, the time has come! Go bring Umm Saeed.' At the crack of dawn, Yasir left the room. The autumn chill cut through his bones. He ran down the alley; it wasn't far. Sumaya had said that Umm Saeed delivered all the newborns of Banu Makhzum and cut their umbilical cords. She slept lightly, alert, so if a labouring woman cried out, she would be there to help. Panting, Yasir stopped and called out, 'Umm Saeed! Come out, my wife, Sumaya...' Umm Saeed stepped onto the porch, but the words she spoke turned Yasir's heart to ashes. She said, 'Go away, man! Leave through the door of this house. I'm not done with my life yet, and I love my children. Just a few days ago, Walid stood right where you are and warned me not to help Sumaya or set foot in your house. Leave and don't come back.'"

Walid's cruelty is beyond anything I can imagine. How could he be so cold to a pregnant woman when Sumaya had never wronged him? After all, Sumaya had nothing to do with him. I fix my gaze on Hababeh's headscarf. "What terrible people. To harm a woman carrying a child is not strength; it is the lowest kind of cruelty. Did the baby come into this world? What did Yasir do?"

"My dear, cruelty and wickedness have existed since the time of Cain and Abel, and they still do. As long as the world keeps turning, good and evil, cruelty and kindness will always exist side by side. Yasir, having lost hope in Umm Saeed, ran toward the house. He had never witnessed a birth before and didn't know what to do. When Sumaya saw Umm Saeed's empty place, she understood what was happening. Crying out in pain, she groaned, 'Warm water.' Yasir hurried to the yard, stacked the firewood, and lit the fire. Every time he breathed on the flames, it was as if he was easing the weight of all the grief inside him. He lowered the bucket into the well once, twice, three times- the blackened pot filled with water. Just as he was about to return to the well, Sumaya's scream pierced the sky. The bucket slipped from Yasir's hands and fell to the ground. He ran back to the room, but there was no sound from Sumaya. Her lips had turned pale, and her sweat-damp hair clung to her forehead. She bit down on the blanket and fainted. Ammar grabbed Sumaya's arms and shook her gently, whispering her name. He lightly slapped her face, but she didn't open her eyes. Yasir broke down into sobs. The thought of losing Sumaya and their child crushed him utterly."

How many have been left voiceless in their pain? How many have been lost to the cruelty of those in power? What difference does it make if it's the ruler of Mecca or Harun? God knows that right here in Baghdad, there are women with no one to hear their cries. Seeing my pain, Hababeh continues, "Don't let grief take hold of your heart, my daughter. Cruel rulers have always existed, and they always will. But God never abandons His servants."

That night, Yasir fought alone until at last the door opened. Umm Saeed appeared in the doorway. She couldn't bear to stay away and had come to help. That morning, with the first light of dawn, the cry of a newborn filled the house. Umm Saeed wrapped the baby in a cloth and placed him in Sumaya's arms, making her promise that no one would ever know she had been there."

I'm thinking of Umm Saeed, of the fear that has taken hold of her. She was a brave woman who went to give help despite Walid's threats.

Voices of a veiled age

Perhaps without her, Sumaya would never have held her child in her arms. I scratch the tip of my nose and crouch on the bed. Hababeh goes on, "Sumaya named her son Ammar. His childhood was much like any other child's. She taught him to be honourable and to carry himself with dignity. Yasir whispered in his ear to never wrong others and to be humble. Against Walid's mockery and cruelty, it was the steady support of Sumaya and Yasir that kept Ammar standing. He grew into a young man with a heart shaped by justice, drawn to beauty and goodness, untouched by what was ugly. You're a mother yourself, and you know how deeply parents shape their children. That good upbringing led Ammar to find the truth sooner than other young men in Mecca. He had come to know the Prophet's ﷺ faith, though neither Sumaya nor Yasir spoke of it. They saw his restlessness but did not know the reason. They thought Walid was tormenting him until Ammar decided to open his heart. That day, Ammar glanced at his mother, at the fine wrinkles around her eyes and at her hair that was no longer brown. He stared at his father's beard, at his bushy white beard, and asked, 'Father, do you remember how whenever I asked you about the poverty of the people, or about the wealth of the idols and their owners, you would nod and say you hoped one day injustice would be wiped away? What about your mother? Does it still hurt your chest to think of girls being buried alive? Are you still afraid of the bloodshed between tribes? Do you remember how much you have been tormented by Walid since day one until now? He still calls me the son of a slave woman. Whenever I am with my friends, he orders me around, and I have no choice but to obey. Do you remember how you always told me not to let sorrow into my heart, to consider myself free, and to trust that Walid would get what he deserves?' Sumaya and Yasir remembered every word clearly. My daughter, people's words come from their beliefs. Beliefs are not like the wind that blows one way today and another tomorrow."

I wet my dry lips. After Hababeh left, I must inform the scribes to write this sentence in beautiful calligraphy: "*A person's belief is not like the wind that blows one way today and another tomorrow.*" I pour sherbet into Hababeh's cup and ask, "What did Ammar say to his family?"

Hababeh wipes her eyes with the corner of her handkerchief and replies, "Ammar said, 'I come from a man whose religious words are much like yours. From Muhammad, Muhammad Amin, the nephew of Abu Talib. He is the Messenger of God. He says idols do no good for the people of this world. He says everyone must worship the one God, seek His help, and follow His laws. Mother! He says women have the same right to live as men, and that burying girls alive is a sin. Black or white, rich or poor, slave or free, all are equal before the one true Lord. I speak of a prophet who taught me to be the lowest before my parents. Do you also wish to meet him? His religion still has fewer followers in Mecca than the fingers on two hands. He is alone.' Sumaya and Yasir were eager to meet the Messenger of God. The next morning, before the sun rose, Ammar led his parents toward a house that smelled of flowers. Meeting Muhammad ﷺ was like finding water after days of running thirsty across the desert for Sumaya and Yasir. It was like finding light while living in complete darkness. Muhammad's ﷺ words captured Yasir and Sumaya's hearts. Their pure nature was drawn to the God of Muhammad and his message. They longed to spend the rest of their lives under his guidance. They didn't just speak of belief. They felt it deep in their souls, and this faith was not for a day or two. Muhammad's ﷺ words were the missing piece in Yasir and Sumaya's lives. Finally, finding that after years of waiting brought them endless peace. Every day, they would spend hours listening to the prophet's words, learning, calming their minds. After all those years, they could finally share their sorrows and find comfort in his speech. In those days, worshipping Muhammad's God was considered a great crime, just as today, loving the descendants of Ali and wanting them is seen as a great offence."

I lower my head. Devotion to the descendants of Ali should be a source of pride, not a reason for people's fear. Woe to Harun and the kings before him who fought against the rightful owners of the time.

"Since you mentioned your love for Harun, I first spoke to you about Sumaya. Sumaya loved her husband far more than you did. You had a grandfather who supported you. Even if Harun had never existed, you would still have lived in comfort. You were the grandchild of the Abbasid household. You had brothers, you had sisters, but Sumaya had only Yasir in the whole world. She was utterly alone, and Yasir's love was all she possessed. Yet she loved her belief even more than Yasir. She could have stayed a worshiper of idols. At the time she and Yasir embraced Muhammad's ﷺ faith, there were fewer Muslims in all of Mecca than the fingers on one hand. Do you know how powerful the owners of the idols were? Do you know how they promoted idol worship? But when she realised the prophet's words were true, she believed in him, and more importantly, she stood firmly by her belief."

I don't look at her. I twist my hair around my finger and bite my lip.

Hababeh clears her throat and continues,

"Every day at dawn, Sumaya woke up with a renewed sense of purpose. She would do her chores and waited for the chance to secretly go with

Yasir to visit the prophet. But one day, her hope for that meeting was crushed. That day, just before noon, she wrapped her hot bread in a cloth and waited for Yasir. When she heard the door open, she grabbed her bundle, thinking it was her husband. But the moment she stepped into the courtyard, she saw Abu Jahl's large, bloodshot eyes. Abu Jahl was one of Mecca's fiercest opponents of the prophet and a close friend of Walid. Sumaya, trembling and confused, tried to say something, but Abu Jahl shouted, 'Bring him here!' Men entered the small courtyard, where the scent of freshly swept earth still lingered. They passed beneath strings of hanging dates and stood before Sumaya. Seeing the scene before her, Sumaya could no longer stand. She dropped to her knees on the ground. The image of Yasir, drenched in blood, his head split open and his collar torn, was burned into her eyes. Sumaya cried out, 'Yasir!' and fainted."

"Oh, poor Sumaya!"

Hababeh coughs, running a hand over her mole. She says, "Sumaya was unconscious when they took her from her house. They pinned her down on the desert sand. When she came to, pain shot through her entire body. Her head felt as heavy as a large copper cauldron. She couldn't breathe. Do you know why? Because, on Abu Jahl's orders, a huge stone was placed on her chest, and also on Yasir's. Imagine the sun of Mecca burning like fire, hot sand underfoot, a massive stone pressing down, and a woman with a delicate body."

I can feel the stone pressing down on my chest just thinking about it. It must have been enormous, impossible to move. If it had been any smaller, Yasir would surely have lifted it to help Sumaya. The thought alone makes it hard to breathe. I wet my lips and ask, "How did Abu

Jahl find out about Somaya and Yasir's faith? And what happened to Ammar?"

"Walid had always been watching them, even in his old age. He saw them visiting the prophet's hideout with their son and reported it to Abu Jahl. As for Ammar, they brought him in an hour later, badly wounded, and tied him to a wooden post."

If I were tied under the sun with a stone on my chest, what could I do? Woe to me forever thinking that living with a man like Harun was the harshest torture!

"Hababeh, tell me, didn't Sumaya complain? Enduring something like that must have been unbearable."

Hababeh shrugs, looks at me for a moment, then fixes her gaze on her hands.

"It was hard, Zubayda. Harder than either of us can imagine. The stone crushed every bone in her chest, but she never gave in. She would say, 'From the very beginning, Muhammad ﷺ warned us this path would be difficult. If the opponents find out about our faith, torture will follow. That day has come now. It's worth it if it means people will find justice. If we want to be free from these stone idols and their masters, we have to endure.' Zubayda, worse than the stone and the heat were the taunts from Walid and Abu Jahl. Every time Abu Jahl came around, he'd step on the stone pressing down on Sumaya's chest, pressing harder, and say, 'Since when did you get so bold? Worshipping Muhammad's unseen God instead of the idols? Haven't you forgotten your days as a servant? Aren't you ashamed of your white hair? If it weren't for Abi Hudhayfah, you'd still be washing the hands and feet of the tribe's men and women. That servant's place was yours.' Yasir would flare up at their insults toward Sumaya, but there was nothing he could do. Then Walid's turn came. He knew Sumaya loved Yasir deeply. He would lash Yasir mercilessly, laughing as he did, saying, 'You should have been my servant, Sumaya. I am far more worthy than Yasir. Look now at the pain he suffers. The power is in my hands.'"

I try to put myself in Sumaya's place for a moment, but I can't. Such strength feels almost unreal to me.

"Hababeh! Was there truly no way out? Was there truly no one who could hear her cries?"

Hababeh clears her throat.

"Yes, Abu Jahl gave Sumaya three choices. He said, 'Either curse Muhammad, or renounce him and his religion, or turn back to your own gods, Lat and Uzza. Then go home and live your life with Yasir.' But Sumaya's lips only repeated, 'There is no God but Allah, and Allah is the Greatest.'"

I stare down at my slippers. Sumaya worshipped God with every fibre of her being. She passed her test with honours. I glance at Hababeh. "I'm not like Sumaya, Hababeh. But I've reached my breaking point. You tell me this story, so I compare myself to her. Maybe I'm not as strong, but I refuse to bow to Harun anymore."

Her kind eyes meet mine. She takes my hand gently and says, "That's not true, Zubayda. I tell you this story and the stories of other women so in the quiet corners of your mind, in your private thoughts, you won't doubt the choice you've made. Remember this, everyone is tested according to the capacity of their own soul. Maybe holding onto your faith here in this grand palace is even harder than keeping it under stones and the scorching sun. How would you know?"

Voices of a veiled age

I give a faint smile and feel a small spark of hope rise inside me. "Do you think I've stayed all these years in the palace for comfort? For jewels and fine robes? No, God is my witness, no. I stay to shield the few Shiites in the city. I stayed to keep Harun's blade of hatred from cutting the Shiites' throats."

"I know, my daughter. I know."

I run my fingers over the wrinkles on the back of her hand, and my thoughts drift toward Sumaya. "Tell me, did all Muslims stand firm under torture like Sumaya? Was there anyone who gave up their faith?"

She smiles and says, "If everyone had been like Sumaya, things would have been easy. In those days, the Muslims were few, and even among them some turned back from their faith. Abu Jahl and the idolaters never let go; if they discovered someone's belief, they destroyed that person's life. Enduring torture required strong faith. On the very first night, Sumaya was jolted awake by the piercing scream of a woman. Her frail body had not withstood the lashes of the whip, and she had fainted. The woman's cries shattered the silence of the night. From the depths of her soul, she screamed, 'Let me go! From now on, I want nothing to do with Muhammad or the God of Muhammad. I do not know him.' By Abu Jahl's command, the soldiers released her. After that, a few others also turned away from the Prophet ﷺ and returned to their homes. Sumaya could have done the same. All it would have taken was one word to say she disowned Muhammad ﷺ, and she would have been freed, along with Yasir and Ammar. She could even have lied, gone home, and worshipped the God of Muhammad in secret. But Zubayda, if she had been afraid, if she had broken under the weight of the stone, if she had given in, do you think anything of Islam would have reached us? If not for Sumayyah's cries, when she declared, 'I believe in the one God of Muhammad. He is the Messenger of God, and I follow his religion.' Would people have dared to take a step against the idols?"

It is true. Sumaya could have spoken against the Prophet and freed herself from torture, but she stayed. She stayed because she knew that her endurance and suffering would stand as proof of the truth.

Hababeh moistens her dry lips, opens her mouth to speak, but a sudden cough seizes her. I hand her a sip of water.

"You don't seem well."

"I'm fine, daughter. I'm fine."

Her faint smile comforts me, then she asks, "Have you ever worn armour? A full suit of iron armour?"

I stare at her, imagining it in this scorching heat, iron armour...

"Each day, the torture grew worse. One day, by Abu Jahl's order, they forced Sumaya and Yasir into heavy iron armour. Yasir had no strength left. He'd open his eyes every few moments, then close them again, gasping from thirst like a fish out of water. The iron armour was like a furnace; a furnace packed with burning coals. As the sun climbed higher, the heat tormented Sumaya more and more. Thick beads of sweat ran down through her hair, tracing a path along her dark waist and flowing down past her toes. She felt herself melting away, bit by bit. She couldn't catch her breath. Her body burned, and her head throbbed with unbearable pain. The salty sweat stung the whip wounds on her skin, and her cries grew louder. Her mind was boiling, and her flesh felt like it was cooking inside that iron cage."

I raise my hand, begging Hababeh to pause.

"Enough, Hababeh. I can't bear this anymore. Tell me, did the Prophet ﷺ ever come to see them? Did he leave them all alone?"

Hababeh's eyes grow sad. She folds her scarf over her lap and says, "Abu Jahl, Walid, and the other leaders of Mecca wouldn't allow the Prophet ﷺ near the prisoners. The only reason they hadn't thrown him into prison was out of respect for his family's lineage. But one day, the Prophet reached them. He gently stroked Yasser's hair, glanced at Sumaya's burnt skin, and spoke words that set Abu Jahl's anger ablaze. The Prophet prayed, 'O God, do not let any of Yasir's family suffer in Your fire and torment.'

That prayer breathed new life into Sumaya."

I think to myself, meeting the Prophet must have been the greatest moment in Sumaya's life. To have the Messenger of God's blessing and prayers; that is the truest happiness.

"What happened in the end? How long did Sumaya hold on?"

Hababeh nervously twists the edge of her scarf. "My dear, Sumaya was strong. Maybe she never showed it on the outside, but inside she had endless strength. Walid took all her power away. He knew Sumaya's life was tied to Yasir's. Every few hours, Walid would come back to torment them. Once, he pressed his foot down hard on Yasir's throat, squeezing with all his might. Yasir's eyes bulged, his face turning purple. Sumaya's cries and screams meant nothing. Walid finally lifted his foot, but after that, no matter how much Sumaya called Yasser's name, there was no answer. She felt the world around her darken; the pain of Yasir's absence was heavier than any stone pressing on her chest. Her heart could not bear it. One of the guards stepped toward Yasir. He shook him. Yasir lay still, like cooked meat inside the iron armour. Walid sneered at Sumaya and said, 'You caused his death, Sumaya. You killed your husband. Yasir is gone. I will not move his body. Let the stench choke you.' Zubayda, Sumaya could still hear Yasir's loving whispers, still remembered his sweet smiles, the first time he looked into her eyes, the first time he bought her clothes, the day he came home tired and saw the burn on the back of her hand from the oven and placed a kiss on the blister. Sumaya's heart was full of sorrow, full of loneliness."

I can no longer hold back my tears. My sobs break free. The worst torture in the world is when your loved one dies beside you, and you think you are to blame. Sumaya, what did they do to you? God, my heart burns at the thought of her grief.

Hababeh's voice trembles, but she whispers,

"The next noon, Yasir's body was still lying on the ground, and Sumaya had forgotten her own pain. Yasir's death gave her the courage to pour all her hatred for Walid, Abu Jahl, and the idols into words. She shouted at Walid and Abu Jahl, 'Your place is in hell. You are made of the same stuff as Satan. On the Day of Judgment, your useless stone idols will be of no help to you. My God is a just God, and He will take our rights from you. Death to you and your gods. If I knew my death would preserve Muhammad's faith, I would give my life willingly.' One day, at last, Sumaya's words ignited the gunpowder in Abu Jahl's soul. He ordered the guards to pull her burned body out of the iron armour. They tied a thick rope to her feet. Each rope was fastened to the leg of a horse."

I sob, and Hababeh's voice grows softer and softer: "By Abu Jahl's order, the horses were driven on. They ran, and Sumaya was dragged over the scorching stones, sometimes toward the black horse, sometimes toward the brown one. She felt as if she were being torn in two, yet she cried out that her God was the God of Muhammad. I think Sumaya's defiance had humiliated Abu Jahl, for suddenly he seized the spear from a guard beside him and ran toward her. He thrust the spear deep into Sumaya's heart, and her blood stained the hot desert sand. Her eyes closed. Ammar cried out, 'Mother... Mother.' But Sumaya was forever silent.

I sink into Hababeh's embrace. I have forgotten my own sorrows. I see only Sumaya, lying among the hot sands of the desert.

4

The sound of the Quran passes through the wooden door of the room and settles in my ear. I take a deep breath and glance at Hababeh. She drinks the water in one gulp and wipes around her lips with the sleeve of her shirt. "Is that the sound of the Quran? Am I hearing it right?" I nod. All my thoughts are with Sumaya, the woman who is like a mountain of patience for me.

"How surprising! I had heard that in Harun al-Rashid's palace, beside the wine cup, a prayer rug is spread and the Quran is recited, but I had never seen it with my own eyes."

I frown.

"Do you see any wine cups here? I started this Quran reading, hoping that God's word would shake the hearts of Harun and his courtiers and make them come to their senses. But alas! Harun is fundamentally opposed to God's word, though when it comes to hypocrisy and pretense, he bows his head in submission. That is why he couldn't oppose what I did. So I read the Quran here alongside these girls, so I won't break under all this oppression and won't bend my back." Hababeh lowers her head and softly says, "I have rarely seen a woman as clever as you."

I wish I weren't so clever, but my husband was a devotee of the Ahl al-Bayt. I wish I had no ears, no tongue, no mind, but my Imam were alive. Hababeh sighs, and I look at her wrinkled hands trembling gently.

Sumaya's memory won't leave me.

She gives me a sweet smile and raises her eyebrow. "Learn from Sumaya, and instead of blaming yourself, pay attention to me. Sumaya did everything she could. Just remember that."

I nod. She's right; I must learn and move on. I stand up and walk toward Henna's cage. Hababeh points to the paintings and poems written on pieces of leather hanging here and there on the walls and asks, "Are these your work too, Lady Zubayda?"

I glance at the walls. I bring out Henna's water pot. It seems the imaginary Zubayda of Hababeh is different from Zubayda, the one devoted to poetry and design. I look at Hababeh's small stature and say, "Yes, they are my work. When I first became Harun's wife, I hoped to use the power of the Quran, poetry, and stories to fight against injustice. I brought together poets and scholars, and since Harun had granted me freedom from worldly concerns, I rewarded them generously with gold to write verses condemning tyranny. I believed that while Harun, the Barmakids, and I might pass away, our poetry would endure, and through it, future generations would come to know us and the times we lived in. I believed that this way I could carry the voice of the oppression of the descendants of Ali to the children in their cradles and to the unborn in their mothers' wombs."

The eyes of Hababeh sparkle. She murmurs under her breath, "May God's blessings be upon you, Lady Zubayda! Your virtues become clearer to me one by one."

I fill the container with water and place it inside the cage. Henna starts making noise, and I continue: "Back then, I thought a good poem was sharper than a sword. Sometimes I told trusted poets to compose verses about the descendants of Ali. They would say that oppression rules here, that Harun knows how to sew mouths shut and break pens."

The sound of the Quran calms my heart. The voice pauses for a moment, then rises again. I recognise the voice. It belongs to a young Persian girl whom Harun gifted to me some time ago, a girl with black hair and beautiful eyes whose recitation of the Quran touches my soul more than anything else.

Hababeh moves toward a fairly large piece of parchment stuck to the wall. On it, a couplet is written in beautiful calligraphy. Squinting, she says, "Do not belittle your work. In an age when people have drifted away from true Islam, sometimes only the language of art can reveal the worth of this jewel. You understood well, my daughter; the audience of poetry is the future. When poetry flows, it serves two purposes. First, it is a scalpel for the asleep; second, it is a sign for the future. Future generations must know that in our time, not everyone was silent. No matter how cruel your husband is, he cannot destroy the decorated pages of poetry about the Ahl al-Bayt hidden in the secret places of homes.

He cannot suppress poetry that is passed down from heart to heart and inspires every pure soul."

I walk toward the bed and lean against the saffron cushion. A cool breeze blows in my heart, but longing burns like fire, turning the garden inside me to ashes. "Your words scatter light into my heart. My being trembles, and I want to rush into Harun's room and disgrace him, but I am no longer that seventeen-year-old Zubayda. Now, people live inside this palace under my protection, shielded by me. Sometimes I wonder what will happen to them if I take any action. This last longing is what brings me to my knees."

Hababeh looks away from the parchment on the wall and gently steps closer to me. The sound of the Quran's recitation has fallen silent. I know that now the girls and women have gathered around Haniyeh and are asking, "Where is Lady Zubayda? Is she unwell?" Then Haniya's hands and feet start to tremble, her cheeks flush with colour, and she doesn't answer their questions. Tonight, they will quietly weave their stories, and until morning, I will be the topic of my maidservants' whispers.

"This Quranic recitation you heard comes from a room where my maidservants gather, more than a hundred of them. They have no one in this world but me. I stand against Harun, but my sisters, my brothers, Fadhl… Harun does not spare them. He knows how deeply I care for those around me and how much I love them."

I sigh quietly and swallow my tears. Since I became the black-clad follower of my Imam, every hour feels like a dark night to me. It's as if the night has been poured into a waterskin with a small hole at the bottom; the night drips down on me, aging my longing and waiting.

Voices of a veiled age

Hababeh takes my face in her hands.

"Your eyes shout the depth of your turmoil. But my dear! Your son Amin, your brother Fadhl, your sisters, your maidservants, your poets, all of them are under God's shield. Have you forgotten this?"

Hababeh still does not know Harun and his courtiers. She is unfamiliar with the palace's unspoken rules. She doesn't realise that they destroy whoever they please, bring down whoever they wish, and scatter their harvest to the wind.

"You don't understand, Hababeh. Do you think those who showed no mercy to Musa ibn Ja'far ﷺ, to the descendants of the Prophet of God, will have mercy on my loved ones? I am not thinking of myself anymore; my heart won't be torn apart any further, but they…"

Hababeh stares into my eyes and asks, "God is holding you now, don't you feel His gentle touch?"

I take my ring off and slip it back on my finger. Once, twice, three times. Hababeh whispers, "The embrace of our Lord is always open to His servant. Do you think Musa ibn Ja'far ﷺ was not held in God's embrace? God's embrace does not mean a person is safe from every harm; it means feeling His approving smile. And our Imam felt that every moment of his life, in the bowing of his prayer, even in Harun's prison… By the way, Zubayda, do you know why your husband decided to imprison Musa ibn Jafar ﷺ? After all, my Imam never harmed him."

Never before have I felt so ashamed upon hearing the word 'your husband' as I do tonight.

I take a deep breath and swallow the air. Remembering those days, the days when Harun intended to imprison the Imam, my whole being trembles. Back then, I wanted to shout and defend the son of Zahra.

Several times, with sweet words, I begged Harun not to harm the Imam. When he came to my room at night, drunk on pure wine, I whispered in his ear, asking him to stop his deeds and fear God. At night, he would listen, but by morning, when dawn broke, he forgot everything. He would see Yahya and his son Ja'far again, hear their words as if by heart, and obey them. Those days, I was like a scarecrow, trying to act but unable to. I sought help from the ministers; sometimes I begged Harun, sometimes I argued, but the result was nothing and nothing.

Hababeh sits beside me, placing her scarf over her head, hiding her white, thinning hair beneath the black cloth. She looks at me. "What happened, daughter? You've drifted into your thoughts." I nod; a tear escapes from the corner of my eye. "It's nothing. Actually, the question you asked has a long story. But I will tell you." Hababeh crouches down on the bed.

"I'm listening, daughter! Tell me."

"When I became a mother, I experienced a unique feeling. Every day and night that I stood over Amin's cradle watching him, I promised myself to raise him with love for the descendants of Ali ﷺ. As he grew taller, my hopes grew bigger. When he reached the age to learn reading and writing, I asked Harun to let me choose a teacher for him myself."

I wanted him to be taught by a man who was a devoted follower of Ahl al-Bayt. Harun agreed. He trusted me and my judgment enough to entrust me with this important task. I was full of joy and excitement. My son was the only one whose lineage traced back to the Hashimites on both Harun's and my side.

Hababeh looks at me, and I see something in the pupils of her eyes.

"No, Hababeh, don't be mistaken. I knew that the caliphate rightfully belonged to Imam Kadhim ﷺ and his descendants. I was certain that Amin should not be the caliph of the Muslims. But... but what did my opinion matter? Harun made Amin his crown prince when he was five years old. As a mother, I wanted my son to carry the love of the descendants of Ali ﷺ in his heart and think in their way."

Hababeh smiles and curls her hand into a fist, trying to hide its trembling.

"I didn't say anything."

"Not your tongue, but your eyes speak."

Hababeh rubs her ankle and suddenly starts coughing, a dry, prolonged cough. I give her water and watch her with concern. She coughs once more and calms down.

"You are Amin's mother; don't tell me your heart has never beat for your son, don't say it has never crossed your mind for him to be crown prince..."

Ashamed, I lower my head. Those days, seeing how much Harun loved Amin filled my heart with joy. I did not want Yahya al-Barmaki or anyone else to push Amin aside and make his half-brother Mamun dear to Harun's eyes.

But one night, I realised my mistake. I understood that the rightful rule was only for the descendants of Zahra. I felt remorse, fell into prostration, and repented. I lift my head, bite my lip, and say, "Once, I was thinking about my son, but I soon realised my error. God knows when I brought Jafar ibn Muhammad ibn Ash'ath to be Amin's teacher, all I cared about was that his beliefs were aligned with the descendants of Ali ﷺ."

Hababeh presses her dry lips together, as if sorting through her thoughts to reach the name Jafar ibn Muhammad ibn Ash'ath. Her eyebrows knit tighter, deepening the furrow between them.

"I have heard his name. As far as I know, he believed in the Imamate of Musa ibn Jafar ﷺ and defended him fiercely."

I brush away a fly circling my head and say to Hababeh, "Yes, he was a Shi'a, but I made an agreement with him not to speak of his beliefs openly in front of Harun, and to teach Amin only what was necessary in the form of lessons. I didn't want Harun to know that my beliefs differed from his. I only hinted that the path to education was open to him and that he should not fear anything. He understood my meaning. Those were good times. Amin spent many hours each day with Ja'far ibn Muhammad. As his mother, I saw his character changing. I asked him to tell me everything he learned. He spoke of the Prophet, the Quran, piety, justice, and sometimes the Imamate. Everything was going well, but then something happened I never expected."

Hababeh moistens her lips. "What happened?"

When I recall Amin's face as a child, sweetly repeating what he had learned to me, I smile. But when I remember his present temperament, a bitter taste fills my mouth.

Harun was pleased with Amin's education. He only ever saw his behaviour and never sat to listen to his words, so he remained unaware of his thoughts. But the palace, the courtiers, Yahya al-Barmaki and his son were another story. Every time I saw Yahya, I could sense his unease; fear flickered in his eyes. Do you know what he was afraid of? That Amin might become caliph, cast him and his family aside, turn to Jafar ibn Muhammad ibn al-Ash'ath, and eventually to Musa ibn Jafar

🕊️, handing the caliphate over to the Imam. He did not want to put his own position and that of his children at risk. After all, his influence over Harun was immense. Harun treated him like the apple of his eye. I thought his worries would come to nothing, but he wove a scheme so dangerous that I learned of it far too late.

Hababeh rests her chin in her hand and leans forward.

"What scheme? What happened? Was Jafar ibn Muhammad cast out?"

I close my eyes for a moment before opening them again.

"I wish that had been it. No, he went for the root, for the Imam himself. When he sensed danger, he turned to the Imam's nephew, Ali ibn Isma'il. He tempted him, filled his head with whispers, and convinced him to come to Baghdad. The money Yahya had already slipped him had left its taste, and the grand promises he offered won him over. Ali ibn Isma'il came to Harun and revealed everything about the Imam, everything he should have kept to himself. He said that Imam Kadhim🕊️ was planning an uprising, that his silence was only a ruse while he secretly gathered an army. He claimed the Imam intended to come to Baghdad soon and seize the throne. He said it over and over until Harun decided to imprison the Imam. That year, Harun went on pilgrimage. In Medina, the Imam and several others came to greet him, but even that did nothing to change his mind. Yahya had filled him with such certainty about the Imam's nonexistent plans that Harun refused to believe my words or see the nobility in the Imam's actions. Harun's eyes were blind, his ears deaf, and if you ask me, his mind was just as closed. In Medina, standing before the Prophet's grave, he said, "O Messenger of God, I ask your forgiveness for imprisoning Musa ibn Jafar, for he intends to divide your people and spill their blood."

Do you see how foolish he is? He thinks he is showing devotion to the Prophet while betraying his descendants. God help me. No matter how I pleaded, no matter how I tried to sway him with wit and charm, nothing worked. My Imam was taken in chains that day, all because of Yahya's malice. After that, Jafar ibn Muhammad ibn al-Ash'ath was removed from teaching Amin.

Hababeh bites her lip, shakes her head, and tightens her grip around her wrist.

"What is it, Hababeh? You look shaken. You told me I should be at ease, that I shouldn't be afraid." I told you, you still don't know the palace. Those who have no mercy for the children of Zahra will have none for those close to me.

Hababeh's frown fades, and a smile gently appears on her lips once more.

"Yes, I still mean what I said. You have to see, among these people, what you are willing to give up to defend your belief, to stand firm in your conviction. Sometimes God tests His closest servants by taking from them their most precious possession. What is yours? Your son? Your brother? I remain silent. What can I say? The words of the heart are not always meant to be spoken. At times, you feel the weight inside you, yet when you try to give it voice, the words will not come. It is as if all the words in existence are too few to carry what you wish to say. How can I tell her that my greatest treasure was my Imam? An Imam who no longer breathes in this world, who was martyred unjustly, in my own city, not far from me, by the hands of someone I once loved. I let out a long sigh, and Hababeh goes on. "Sometimes a person's most precious possession is their life. Sometimes it is their family. Sometimes it is the hand that writes. If a person can give up their most precious thing for God and for their Imam, that is devotion. Do you want me to tell you another story?"

I nod.

"Yes, tell me. But Hababeh, what if time runs short, and you go before I understand your secret?"

Hababeh laughs, scratches the small mole on her cheek, and leans back against the pillow.

"These stories are part of my great secret. Until you hear them, you will never believe what my secret truly is."

◆

I pull my knees to my chest, smooth the fabric of my black dress, and fix my eyes on her. She clears her throat. "Have you ever heard the name Qanwa? She was a small, wheat-skinned girl with thin hair and a long face. She had been born before her time, and her tiny frame was the result. She carried a heavy grief in her heart; Qanwa never saw her mother. One long spring afternoon, the pains came to her mother, and no matter what the midwife did, she could not stop the bleeding. The cry of newborn Qanwa filled the house, and her mother's breath fell silent forever. The father was left with a hungry baby girl, wrapped in a sheet, her tiny face and head still streaked with blood. There was no mother's embrace to calm Qanwa, only her father's hands and his worried eyes. Raising a daughter alone isn't easy. You have to work to put food on the table, feed the baby, change her, and keep her clean. But Qanwa's father did it all, completely. At night, he would cry from exhaustion and loneliness, yet he never allowed his little girl to feel the absence of her mother, though the weight of that absence was always with her. I remember my own childhood, the days when only my mother's touch could bring me peace, when I could fall asleep only in her arms. Nothing is harder than tearing a mother and daughter apart. I wet my dry lips and ask, "Who was Qanwa's father?"

Hababeh squeezes her trembling hand, coughs softly, and says, "She was the daughter of Rushayd al-Hajari, a friend and confidant of our first Imam, Ali ibn Abi Talib ﷺ. Rushayd would sit with the Imam, listening to his words, speaking of what was on his mind, and drawing strength from the comfort they gave him. He was a Shi'a, and he passed his faith on to Qanwa. She was a quiet, little, shy girl. She had no companions but her father, yet the moment she heard the name of Ali ﷺ, her hands would tremble, and her heart would race. The greatest joy in her life was hearing her Imam's words. From the time she was small, Rushayd would sit her on his knee and tell her about Imam Ali ﷺ and Fatima al-Zahra ﷺ, about their kindness and their goodness. When he pushed her on the swing, when he fed her, when he stayed awake through the night by her side while she had a fever, when he braided her hair, he spoke of Ali ﷺ and the truth of his Imamate. Qanwa grew, and soon suitors began to come, but she refused them all."

My tongue moves quickly as I ask, "But why?" Hababeh stretches out her leg, her hand trembling more; I can feel it. "The reason was her father. For Qanwa, her father meant everything. He was her whole life, her only joy and attachment. In short, her most precious treasure."

Voices of a veiled age

My palm sweats, and I wipe my hand on my shirt. "Qanwa's greatest treasure was her father. Don't tell me she stayed at the end of this story, having to choose between... between..." Hababeh takes my hands in hers, squeezing my fingers tight. "This is Qanwa's choice. The life of a girl who loved her father deeply and had no one else in this vast world but him. The same father who taught her that love for Ali ﷺ and faith in his family are above all else in this world. Qanwa was the devoted daughter of her father, Lady Zubayda."

Speaking becomes hard for me. My hands clench, and I know I look pale. Choices shape a person's destiny, and oh, the weight of difficult choices when you feel trapped between two paths. And being stuck between those paths gets even harder when the choice is between two parts of yourself, between your worldly love and your love for the hereafter. Crossroads are the only places where people show whether they truly live what they say. And soon, I will prove that I am Zubayda, devoted to the descendants of Ali ﷺ.

"Keep going, Hababeh, tell me about Qanwa's crossroads and her choice."

Hababeh fixes her gaze on the Quran wrapped in silk on the shelf and murmurs, "Don't think this suffocation and oppression is only for your time. I have seen days when speaking of Ali ibn Abi Talib ﷺ, talking about the Prophet's children, was a harsh punishment, worse than you can imagine. Rushayd knew our master Ali's ﷺ words by heart; he taught them to Qanwa. She tried to connect with the women and girls around her. It was hard. When she spoke, her tongue would tie itself in knots. People laughed at her. She would shrink and tremble, but because she felt it was her duty to deliver the Imam's message to the women, she bore the pain. Her father warned her; sometimes Qanwa listened, sometimes she didn't. She knew her father approved of her mission deep down, and only fatherly concern made him sometimes stop her from speaking. After all, Rushayd himself never spared any effort to bring Ali's ﷺ words to the people, and that very effort stirred the anger of Ubaidullah ibn Ziyad."

I rub my eyes. My head feels heavy, as if a large copper pot has been set on it, and the water inside is constantly boiling.

I say, "I always wonder, since Ubaidullah was so close to Imam Ali ﷺ, how did the people back then fail to tell right from wrong?"

Hababeh nods slowly, twisting the edge of her handkerchief around her finger. "If a person doesn't build themselves from within, desires for wealth, status, and comfort will consume them. Ubaidullah attracted people in different ways. People prefer wealth, ease, and security, even if it comes with oppression. True justice and the rule of genuine faith don't sit well with many because their worldly interests are at risk. This isn't just a story of today or yesterday. Since the time of Prophet Noah, Abraham the Friend of God, and Joseph the Prophet, there have always been those trying to hide the sun of truth behind clouds of deceit and hypocrisy, using the shadow to serve their own interests.

Ubaidullah opposed the descendants of Ali ﷺ more than anyone else. He wanted to dry up the roots of love and loyalty to the master. Rushayd and others like him stood in his way. After all, pure hearts awaken when they taste even a sip of the sea, and the sayings Rushayd shared from our master were like that healing sip. But one day, Ubaidullah decided to silence Rushayd's voice.

That day, Rushayd had stoked the oven, and Qanwa was rolling out dough to bake bread when the door with four panels swung open, and Ubaidullah's soldiers filled their small courtyard. The dough slipped from Qanwa's hands; a lump tightened in her throat. Her whole body trembled. She knew how the story would end."

I furrow my brow and ask, "What do you mean? How did Qanwa know?"

Hababeh lays her trembling hand on her knee. She lets out a soft cough, then starts to speak:

"Our master Ali ﷺ had told Rushayd how he would be martyred and what Ubaidullah would do to him. Rushayd passed those words from the Imam ﷺ on to Qanwa so that she would be ready for the destined day. The descendants of Ali know the unseen, dear Zubayda. That day, the soldiers took Rushayd and Qanwa to Ubaidullah. He sat on his throne, surrounded by beautiful young girls. Ubaidullah had no intention of killing Rushayd; he only wanted to force him, by any means, to speak ill of Ali ﷺ and his family. That's why he summoned Qanwa close with flattering words. He examined her and motioned for her to come nearer. Then, quietly into her ear, he said, 'Everyone says Rushayd has nothing in this world but you, and you have nothing but your father. They say your father obeys you and can't bear to see you cry. You know I've called you here for punishment today… but your innocent face moves me. I want to give you a chance. If you love your dear father and don't want to see him suffer, go to him now and ask him to curse Ali a few times and to stop telling his stories. Then, out of my own grace, I will spare him.' Qanwa looked at Ubaidullah with frightened eyes and saw her six-year-old self reflected in his pupils. Do you know why Qanwa's tongue was so tied? A bitter and terrifying memory from when she was six darkened her. The memory of the day their door was kicked open and the soldiers of the ruler stormed in. The day she saw her father's face bruised and wanted to scream. Wanted to let out the termites gnawing at her mind, but like a lifeless piece of meat, she fell from the swing to the ground, her mouth filled with the salt of blood and the bitterness of dust. Before her eyes, the soldiers began to beat her father. One stabbed him in the side with a bayonet, and another crushed his face. The soldiers drew their lines and warned that Rushayd must stop aiding Ali and mind his own affairs. As they were leaving that day, one soldier knelt in front of Qanwa, a wide grin spreading across his face, revealing yellowed teeth, and shouted, 'Rushayd! If you keep this up, I'll slit your head from ear to ear right in front of your precious little girl.' That day, the lingering scent of a damp cloth hit Qanwa's face, and silent tears rolled down her cheeks. The soldiers were gone, but no matter how hard she tried, she couldn't call out her father's name. Her mind kept replaying the soldier's face, the knife in his hand, and her father's head severed from his body. From that day on, Qanwa's tongue faltered, and the stutter never left her."

I see Qanwa before my eyes, a girl with chestnut hair, wearing a ruffled dress, and wide, startled eyes. She was just six years old, her tongue tied and tears quietly slipping down her cheeks. I set that image aside, lean forward, and softly place my hand on Hababeh's knee. "Surely Qanwa was terrified when she faced Ubaidullah and heard his threats, just like those childhood days."

Hababeh nods. "Yes, an unimaginable fear gripped her soul. That day, Qanwa saw herself in Ubaidullah's eyes. Frustrated by her trembling, fixed gaze, Ubaidullah stomped the ground and shouted, 'What's the matter, mad girl? What do your eyes want from me? Go away and tell your father what I said.' Qanwa stepped back from Ubaidullah. She was no longer six; she was twenty-six and constantly wondered what the sum of those twenty-six years of her life truly was?"

Hababeh's cough interrupts her before she can finish, her face pale, skin the colour of moonlight, cold and white. I squeeze her hand gently. "Are you alright, Hababeh? Should I call a doctor? Let me help you get better."

She shakes her head.

"No, my time is breaking like glass. No doctor can heal this pain. Let me make the most of every minute tonight."

I fall silent, fill her glass with water, and hand it to her. "Here, wet your throat."

She takes a sip, leans her head against the wall, and lets her eyelids close. "Sometimes, you have to choose between yourself and God. It's hard, but that's what separates humans from other creatures. Animals follow instinct, but humans have a choice: to be angelic or beastly. Free will is a great gift from God, but it also puts us to a difficult test. I think Qanwa's struggle was harder than most. After all, a father is a daughter's refuge and strength. When you have a father, it feels like the whole world is by your side. His voice, his gaze, his gentle touch, his stern look, even his breath comforts your heart, chasing away sorrow and filling you with peace. To willingly, by your own choice, push your father toward absence, is a heavy, crushing burden."

I curl up inside myself, wanting to close my eyes and return to childhood, the days when I had a father. But what did he look like? Was he thin? Tall? Did his gaze hold kindness or not? What scent did his body carry? Were his hands warm or cold? I don't know. And if he had thirsted for the blood of Zahra's children as Harun did, what would I have done? I wish I weren't of the Abbasid line. I wish I didn't carry their name alongside mine. Oh, fate, why did you make me open my eyes in such a family?

Hababeh glances at me from the corner of her eye. I release her hand and lean back against the pillow.

"Tell me the rest. What did Qanwa do?"

Hababeh's gaze falls on the slippers lying by the bed. "The death of Qanwa's father meant only one thing: loneliness. You don't know what loneliness truly means, especially for a girl without fists or a voice. Her father was like water to her, like air. But she did not want to leave the community alone and keep her father safe. When Ubaidullah shouted, Qanwa stepped toward her father, trembling, not from the shout, but from the weight of the words she was about to say. The soldiers stepped aside, and her father's lips kept moving in prayer. Qanwa felt as if the walls of Ubaidullah's palace trapped her inside. She felt the ceiling collapsing over her head, struggling to breathe. When her father saw her tear-filled eyes, he smiled, a bitter smile. Qanwa knelt before him, placed her hands on his shoulders, and leaned in close.

'I looooove you, faaaather, but Ali is the leader of the nation and you are his follower.'

A soldier who heard Qanwa's whisper aimed his spear at her and pushed her away. Ubaidullah burst into loud laughter and said, 'Arrogance runs in your blood. You are unworthy, unworthy of mercy and opportunity.'

Rushayd, now certain of Qanwa's loyalty, cleared his throat and shouted, 'I'll say the last word first. My master Aliﷺ told me how I would be martyred at your hands. So, hurry and sentence me to torture. I'm waiting for you to fulfil my master's words. Then even the blind to the truth will believe that my master knew the unseen and was the guardian of God.' Ubaidullah rose, paced the room, and spat toward Rushayd. He yelled, 'You fool! Even if I die today, I won't let Ali's words come true.' At that, Qanwa ran toward her father, but a soldier grabbed her arm and dragged her away toward the exit. At the palace doorway, Qanwa clawed at the ground, the soldiers' spears cutting her side. Then, by Ubaidullah's command, a man entered the hall carrying a gleaming, sharp sword, its shine blinding Qanva's eyes. Ubaidullah smirked and nodded. Without looking at Qanwa, the man with the stone face cut off Rushayd's hands and feet. Qanwa knew her back would no longer straighten; she knew she was no longer alive. She saw her father being torn apart, and her scream reached the back of her throat and choked. Tears wouldn't stop, and Ubaidullah's smiling eyes turned her to ashes. But Rushayd was still alive. Qanwa's father still breathed and whispered prayers."

A single tear dripped from my eye onto my lap. I didn't look at Hababeh, but I felt her choking back tears.

"Ubaidullah took cruelty to its limit; he ordered Qanwa to carry her bloodied father out of the palace alone. The entire hallway, all the way to Ubaidullah's throne, was soaked with blood, deep red. Trembling in every part of her being, Qanwa lifted her father onto her shoulders. Her father did not cry out, but his blood poured onto Qanwa's clothes, and she felt herself melting from the warmth of his blood. At the palace exit, people stood watching. They began to rush toward Qanwa and

Rushayd, and the pressure of the crowd grew heavier by the moment. Qanwa glanced at the crowd, thinking she carried a heavy responsibility, as if she had just been born anew. She shouted, 'We are the followers of Ali ibn Abi Talib ﷺ. He was the rightful Imam and had foretold that Ubaidullah would cut off my father's hands, feet, and tongue.' At her words, the crowd pressed in even tighter. Rushayd, unable to believe Qanwa was speaking without stammering, whispered, 'My daughter… you… you…' Qanwa herself did not understand why or how her tongue was suddenly free. She nodded slightly, trying to reassure her father, but as Rushayd's voice grew louder, so did the roar of the crowd.

'So your master was lying? … he can actually speak.'

'Then Ali's words were just dreams and fantasies…'

Hearing this, Rushayd began reciting hadiths about Ali ﷺ, his virtues, his good deeds, and his unmatched sermons. The people listened intently until soldiers parted the crowd and advanced toward them. Qanwa heard their footsteps, but before she could react, a soldier kicked her from behind. Pain shot through her body. She dropped to her knees as Rushayd fell to the ground. A soldier sat on Rushayd's chest and pulled his tongue out by the throat. In the blink of an eye, the soldier cut Rushayd's tongue and shouted, 'By Ubaidullah's order, anyone who speaks of Ali ﷺ must have their tongue cut out from the root.' The terrified crowd, eyes wide in shock, stepped back from Qanwa, who stared down at Rushayd, and from Rushayd himself, lying helpless and limbless on the ground like a piece of meat. The soldiers began moving back toward the palace, but Qanwa's voice stopped them in their tracks. She shouted, 'From now on, I am my father's voice. I am Qanwa bint Rushayd, a follower of Ali ibn Abi Talib ﷺ.'"

I hug my knees tightly and press my chin against them. Sometimes, a person reaches a point where they feel smaller than anyone else, weaker and more fragile. That feeling drips into your heart bit by bit; your whole being aches from accepting it, as if a blacksmith's heavy hammer is pounding down on you, crushing your body with each blow. At times like this, I just want to sleep, silent, thoughtless. Then, when I wake up the next morning, I shake myself free and try to erase that deadly belief from my memory and heart. But this time, there is no room for sleep. I think only of destruction, of everything falling apart.

Hababeh stares silently at the painting at the end of the room, the worn hands of an artist holding a thin brush between his fingers.

"Hababeh, what happened to Qanwa? Can a person really endure so much pain? How can she close her eyes to her father's suffering and calm her heart?"

She slowly turns her head, her eyes heavy with tiredness and shimmering with unshed tears.

"A person can be stronger than you think. A person can make the impossible possible. Zubayda, who painted this?"

I find myself looking at the painting on the wall. It was done by one of the palace painters, an old, thin man with greying hair and thick eyebrows. The day after I gathered all the poets, writers, and painters to urge them to reveal the truth, he came to me. His eyes were red and troubled, showing he had endured a difficult night.

I take my eyes off the painting and turn to Hababeh. "I don't know him well. He was a grey-haired painter. One morning, he came to me and said that the hands that hold a pen for truth and endurance are sacred. He said he believed I was a supporter of those sacred hands and that he stayed awake all night to paint this for me as a gift. A few days later, I heard that Harun had him imprisoned and poisoned. I don't know why... but he must have opposed the caliph. You know Harun has no mercy."

Hababeh stands quietly and moves slowly toward the painting, coughing dryly. "Sacred hands…"

I put on my slippers and walk over to her.

"What is it, Hababeh?"

"Do you remember when I said people are tested through their most precious possessions?"

I nod. "How could I forget? Your words stay with me."

She sighs, trembling hand reaching out to me. "That painter was right. Hands are sacred. On Judgment Day, those very hands will testify that I held the stone of Imamate like a precious treasure and served the descendants of Ali ﷺ."

I take her hand in mine; her fingers are warm. I want to say something, but she keeps going: "But there are hands even more sacred," she said softly. "Hands that wrote down the words of the Imam ﷺ so they would be remembered. Hands that were cut off for recording the sayings of the Prophet's family, destroyed without mercy."

I turn my eyes away from the fine wrinkles at the corners of Hababeh's eyes and fix them on the painting. Two hands fill the page, one holding a pen, the other an inkwell. The arms are drawn up to the elbows. I'm about to ask a question, but a knock at the door and Haniya's voice interrupt me.

"Khatoon, when should I bring dinner?"

Voices of a veiled age

I haven't eaten since noon. Hababeh must be hungry too; I can't tell if she's had a single bite since dawn. Haniya is still standing in the doorway, and the smell of roasted lamb drifts in. Since the day I heard of Musa ibn Jafar's ﷺ martyrdom, I've had no appetite. Whatever I force down turns in my stomach within moments, and I end up bringing it back up.

"Wait a little, then bring it," I tell her.

Haniya bows her head and leaves.

Hababeh is staring at the painting. I can't tell what she sees in it that escapes me. "What do you mean, Hababeh? Which sacred hands? What destruction? Has Harun done something I don't know about?"

She smiles. "No, my dear, no. Harun has nothing to do with this. I'm talking about Umm Khalid. Tell me, can you bear to hear another story?"

I nod.

"I'm all ears, if you still have the breath to tell it."

She smiles.

"Don't worry about me. I have more strength than the old women in your palace."

I like her sweetness, the sly charm in her words, like sugar on the tongue. Hababeh lets out a sigh and turns her gaze away from the painting. "Many believe women are weak by nature. But I think women can change the fate of many lives. Zubayda, women, these delicate beings whose hearts are as fragile as a crystal vase can be as strong as steel, and give that strength to others.

───── ✦◆✦ ─────

I want to tell you the story of Umm Khalid. A tall, broad-shouldered woman, chaste and bold. Men never saw her face, yet the sound of her words of truth reached the ears of the world, and the hadiths she wrote will remain as long as the world stands."

I place my hand on Hababeh's back and feel the sharp outline of her bones; her skin clings to them, with not a scrap of flesh left. I lead her to the bed. She sits on the edge while I remain standing in front of her. "Umm Khalid lived in the time of Imam Sadiq ﷺ. She was a Shia, a true Shia. She wrote down hadiths and passed on the Imam's words. Her courage and faith came from her mother's upbringing, a mother with the heart of a lion, who, every time she put her breast to her daughter's lips, was feeding her lessons in endurance. Umm Khalid's father was martyred when she was a child, killed by one of the rulers of the time. His name… his name… my memory fails me, my dear. But I know well that he, too, gave his life for the descendants of Ali ﷺ."

I sit on the bed, leaning back against the pillow. How fortunate Umm Khalid is, for her father was Shia, and so was her mother. But me… I have been different from her all my life. From the time I first opened my eyes, with every bite of bread, every sip of water, every touch of affection, those around me poured their hatred of the Shia into my heart.

Hababeh shifts closer and rests her hand on my knee, which I'm holding to my chest. I lift my head. She smiles, showing her teeth. One is missing, the one next to her canine.

Voices of a veiled age

"Do you want to keep spinning your thoughts like this? Or would you rather hear the rest of the story and learn more about Umm Khalid before you put yourself on one side of the scale and her on the other?"

I bite my lip and draw my knees closer. How did she know? "I didn't say anything. Go on, tell me about Umm Khalid."

She leans back, scratching the mole on her cheek. "All right. If only you knew, your eyes are like clear mirrors. Whatever's on your mind shows itself there."

My cheeks flush, and I twirl my ring around my finger. Hababeh raises her thin brows and smiles. "Finished with your thoughts?"

"My thoughts never end, Hababeh. My conscience aches. My soul is in constant torment. It's like an arrow lodged in my heart, a bone caught in my throat. When I realised what Harun intended, when I saw he was bent on destroying Musa ibn Jafar ﷺ. I should have done something. But I did nothing... I sat there like a child who has watched her mother die before her eyes and couldn't even cry out."

"My daughter, you're torturing yourself. This family has suffered enough. You couldn't have stood alone against Harun."

I could have. I should have done something... I should have... I push the thoughts swirling in my head aside and meet her eyes. "Tell me, Hababeh. Let me go and speak of Umm Khalid. My heart will not rest as long as I'm trapped in this black palace."

"All right, my daughter. I know how you feel. I'll tell you about Umm Khalid. Her father was an honourable man, but when he died, he left neither money for his wife and child nor a roof over their heads. He even died in debt. The earth had barely covered his grave when men stood over his wife and daughter, demanding repayment. Fear filled them both. Loneliness is bitter, but to be abandoned in your hour of greatest need, with no one to help you, is far worse. When you lose a loved one, you need comfort, someone whose words can soothe your grief and wipe away your tears. Umm Khalid and her mother had no one. Instead, on top of their mourning, they were forced to wrestle with hardship after hardship, more than they could bear. In that cold graveyard, as the winter wind slapped Umm Khalid's flushed cheeks, something happened, something that at first seemed like good fortune, but proved to be a great test."

I pick up an apple from the bowl, red and juicy. One of the poets Harun had executed yesterday left behind a small child, I think a five-year-old girl. I had pleaded with him: if you cannot spare the father's life, then at least have mercy on the mother for the sake of that child. But he would not listen. When he had the poet and his wife executed, only then did his ears hear and his eyes see. His throat tightened, and he gave the order: 'Bring the girl to the palace so she may grow up under Harun al-Rashid's protection and never feel the absence of her parents.' I wanted to spit in his face. Maybe he saw the hatred in my eyes, because he quickly brushed away his tears and finished his wine.

Hababeh rubs her eyes and goes on. "In that same cemetery, Umm Khalid's uncle settled his debts. The creditors left, and Umm Khalid's mother wanted to fall at her brother-in-law's feet in gratitude, but then she heard something that set her whole being on fire. The man was saying he had paid the debts in exchange for marrying Umm Khalid's mother, and that now she and the girl must move into his house. For a woman, it is hard to give herself into the hands of someone who has no desire for her, especially just hours after her husband's death. Umm

Khalid's uncle was nothing like her father. Her father was a Shiite; her uncle was not. Her father never drank wine; her uncle was a drunkard. Her father kept his distance from the caliph and the rulers of the day; her uncle shared their table and their cups. Umm Khalid and her mother left a clean and simple life for a grand house filled with music, dancing, and wine. At night, her mother would hold her tightly until morning, whispering verses from the Qur'an into her ear. She told her of the Prophet, of Ali's ﷺ bravery, of Hasan's ﷺ exile, of the desert of Karbala. Then she would tell her the story of Ruqaya, the story of Sakina, and finally the story of Lady Zaynab. And she would ask her daughter, 'My precious one, do you wish to be the Zaynab of your time?' The little girl would give a wholehearted 'yes' and drift off to sleep. Childhood was a good season of life, until the day Umm Khalid's bones began to stretch, her frame grew tall as a cypress, and her womanly beauty began to show. That was when her uncle set his plans in motion. The palace was not short of men who longed for a life with a girl like Umm Khalid. She had not only height and striking eyes, but also a sharp tongue and a gift for speech. The men of the court, weary at times of their own wives, gentle as lambs, would find themselves craving a woman as strong-willed as Umm Khalid…"

I smirk and lace my fingers together. Umm Khalid, I wish you knew I understand your pain. I am a woman; I know the torment of being treated as a plaything for men's amusement, of being seen as a puppet on their stage.

I hold out a small slice of apple to Hababeh. "So? Did Umm Khalid give in to her uncle's wishes?"

Hababeh tucks her legs beneath her and takes the apple from my hand. "No. Umm Khalid stood at a crossroads. Her uncle had chosen for her an old man, one of the caliph's advisers. That man was the uncle's way into the halls of power, and by offering Umm Khalid to him, he hoped to secure his own place in the hearts of the courtiers. The uncle's word was final: marry the old man or leave the house and face the streets alone. He pressed her, taunted her, until she chose the second path. She would not give herself to her uncle's scheme, nor marry a man who was the sworn enemy of the descendants of Ali ﷺ."

My teeth sink into the flesh of the apple, its sweetness spreading through my mouth. Umm Khalid refused her uncle's proposal, but I chose to be with a man who was an enemy of the descendants of Ali. Curse me and the love I had at seventeen. Hababeh lets out a long yawn. "Where are you, my girl? Where does your mind wander off to and back from?"

I manage a faint smile at that. "Go on… tell me what happens next, before Haniya comes in with the tray of food."

"All right, all right. Umm Khalid had no choice but to tie up her bundle. Her mother was in tears, but she was certain she had to leave." "Leave? Where to? Did she have a home of her own?"
"No, my girl. She had nowhere, except for the home that is the hope of us all. We have no place to go but to the house of the Prophet's family. And Umm Khalid was no different. She went to the door of Imam Sadiq's ﷺ house."

I glance at the apple slices left in the dish. She goes on. "Many times, before she was driven from her home, Umm Khalid had sat in Imam Ja'far Sadiq's ﷺ presence, listening to his words. In her uncle's grand house, in a city where most women were caught up in their daily routines, Umm Khalid struggled to find her way to the Imam. While others thought of dresses and jewels, or the price of onions and a pot of rich stew, she would sit and listen to him. That day her heart was in turmoil, but with perfect respect she told him of her misfortune. She thought the Imam might give her a gift, perhaps a few dinars to help her get by. But the Imam's generosity was far greater than she had ever imagined."

This family is like a generous sky, pouring down kindness upon the earth and time without end. Their love spreads to others. In contrast, Harun is unmatched in greed, cruelty, and deceit, and his oppression stings the people of this land like a venomous bite. Hababeh closes her eyes and whispers, "The Imam ﷺ bought a small house for Umm Khalid, a home with the basic necessities. It was after that moment that Umm Khalid began sharing the teachings of Imam Sadiq ﷺ. I think she no longer feared anything. All the days she lived in her uncle's house, she was afraid someone would find out she was writing down the Imam's sayings and that her mother would be harmed. But now... now that she had left that house and was no longer under their yoke, now that, by the Imam's ﷺ grace, she had a home, she wanted with all her heart to be the Imam's ﷺ voice. In those days, speaking the truth was difficult, just as it is now. And perhaps, with Yusuf ibn Omar, the governor of Iraq, it was even harder."

Hababeh starts coughing. The cough won't stop. She covers her mouth with a handkerchief. The coughs come dry and one after another. When she lowers the cloth, there's a spot of blood on it.

"Hababeh, are you all right? That blood... let me call a doctor."

She folds the handkerchief and wipes her face.

"It seems you've forgotten this is Harun's palace and I am a Twelver Shiite. A doctor here would poison me instead of healing me, my dear girl."

She says the last line with a laugh. I furrow my brows.

"You've forgotten, too, that I am still a lady of this palace. I have connections and my own people."

Hababeh shakes her head gently. I lean back and hug my knees.

"My health is fine. When I'm with you, and I share my secret, I feel better... Let me finish Umm Khalid's story. Every day, Umm Khalid sat listening to Imam Sadiq's ﷺ words. The Imam looked upon her with great respect. Once, men had gathered around the Imam ﷺ, all ears waiting to hear his speech. But the Imam ﷺ said nothing. Then the door opened, and Umm Khalid entered. One of the eyewitnesses to that gathering told me about it. He said, 'We saw the Imam ﷺ smile when Umm Khalid arrived and asked, "Do you wish to hear Umm Khalid speak?" We nodded, but some of the men frowned. Arab men never accepted the superiority of a woman over themselves, but at the same time, they didn't want to speak against the Imam.' My witness said, 'We all turned to Umm Khalid's lips. She opened her mouth, and her words left us speechless. The Imam asked her about leadership, and Umm Khalid spoke eloquently and with grace. We were amazed.'"

I smile. I admire strong women, those who refuse to let men play with their lives.

Hababeh scratches the tip of her nose and shifts slightly. "After Umm Khalid escaped her uncle's house and settled in a home arranged by the Imam's servant, she married a Shiite man. Living alone was hard, especially in Iraq. Every time Umm Khalid stepped outside, ten pairs of eyes watched her... Marrying a man who loved Imam Sadiq ﷺ put an end to all the gossip and stares... but it seemed Umm Khalid still had more tests to face. A few months after their marriage, her husband was martyred. The soldiers of the governor of Iraq killed him while he was spreading Shiism in a bathhouse. At that time, Umm Khalid was pregnant. When she heard the news of her husband's martyrdom, she felt orphaned once again."

Raising a boy without a father must have been difficult. Amin still prefers his father's company above all else. When I see him standing shoulder to shoulder with Harun, hanging on his every word, I feel more ashamed than ever. Sometimes, the thought that I am Amin's mother, the next caliph, feels even heavier than being Harun's wife.

I rest my chin on my hand. "Before hearing Umm Khalid's story, I thought she was a happy and peaceful woman. But now..."

She laughs softly. "God tests people according to their capacity. No two people have the same measure. Umm Khalid could endure every pain and suffering, stumble, and rise again. It seems God has made a woman's heart bigger, as if women can more easily accept the wounds of the heart and stand tall. I don't know, but I think only one thing can break down a woman's strong fortress, and that is love. Umm Khalid was strong and steady in the eyes of everyone, a scribe and narrator of hadith in front of her late husband. But in front of Zayd, she became like a calm and innocent child. Just as you are the Lady Zubayda to everyone, but once in front of Harun, you lost your heart..."

She's right: love, as much as it empowers, can also weaken you. It makes you fragile, vulnerable. But I no longer want to be known by my love for

Harun. For a long time now, my heart has held no love. I have to wipe away the stain this love has left.

"Hababeh! My love for Harun has turned into hatred. I have no desire to remember those days of passion. For years, I lived hoping Harun would change, hoping his hands wouldn't be stained with the blood of the best servant of God. But day by day, he grew worse, his cruelty and arrogance grew stronger; he kept the light of the Imam ﷺ away, took bread and water from him, threw the Imam into damp prisons that never saw sunlight, and left me longing for just one meeting. This man is the devil himself, and I refuse to ever be known by my love for him."

Hababeh nods, her eyes shining. "Well said, my daughter! May God and the Ahl al-Bayt bless you! Your words show you love, but the children of Zahra."

I squeeze her hand.

"Aren't you going to tell me the rest of Umm Khalid's story?"

Hababeh taps gently on the crystal glass with her agate ring. "Yes, I was about to tell you about Umm Khalid's love. Some time after her husband's death, she met Zayd, and from the very first moment, like an inexperienced girl, she fell for him. Zayd and Umm Khalid intended to be joined in marriage. By the way, do you know Zayd?"

"I've heard the name. Honestly, the stories you tell sound familiar, but you tell them so sweetly it feels like a brand-new tale."

Hababeh wipes her lips with her handkerchief and says, "I know, but I want you to hear everything in all its details, again, in one night. Zayd was the son of Ali ibn Husain and the grandson of Husain ibn Ali, the grandson of Imam Husain ﷺ. Zayd rose up against the Umayyad rule. But Yusuf ibn Omar, the governor of Iraq, never gave him the chance to organise his uprising. I always wonder what might have happened if Zayd's rebellion had succeeded. Maybe our Imam's ﷺ bones wouldn't have softened in that dark prison. Maybe he wouldn't have died from poison born of hatred. Maybe the people could have benefited from his presence..."

I want to say something, but she continues with a smile, "And maybe I wouldn't be here now, and I would never have met you. But it didn't happen... Zayd and his followers were defeated in battle against the Umayyads. His uprising had awakened the silent people. But the governor of Iraq wanted to silence all voices. The thirst for power and the throne can turn a person into a monster. Yusuf became such a monster to protect his position and his throne. He beheaded Zayd. Then, to intimidate the people and crush other opponents, he ordered Zayd's head to be displayed high on the gate of Damascus. Passersbys would tremble at the sight of Zayd's head and dared no longer speak a word against the Ummayyads..."

I shift slightly on the bed. "Love came uninvited to Umm Khalid's heart, but she was a witness to the falling of her beloved before they could be united."

Hababeh straightens her back and lets out a soft sigh before continuing: "Yes. Every day, she died and came back to life, seeing Zayd's body at the city's gate. But she did not lose herself. She never forgot her mission. She remembered what Zayd had given his life for... Right in the height of oppression, when men hid in the city's shadows, Umm Khalid, with a heart full of hatred for the Ummayyads and love for the Ahl al-Bayt, carried Imam Sadiq's words to the people, so the truth would live on, so that the people would recognise the rightful Imam."

I admire her. In my heart, I praise her strength and steadfastness. I scratch the bridge of my nose and toy with my ring. I fix my gaze on Henna's cage, on her, sitting on the wooden perch inside, dozing off. "If I were in her place, I would have stayed home, spending my days crying and mourning. Before the Imam's martyrdom, I was just another Zubayda."

Hababeh smiles and squeezes my hand. "That's not true, Lady Zubayda! You underestimate yourself. Or maybe you're just humble. Haven't you stood up to Harun more than once? Your situation is not the same as Umm Khalid's. You're smart, and so far, you haven't let Harun's schemes succeed. You've always been there to protect the Shia. Surely God saw something in you to place you here, in this palace full of light and colour. Do you think it's easy not to fall for all this wealth and power?"

It's good to have Hababeh by my side, never withholding her words, knowing just how to soothe my pains.

"Don't you want to hear the rest of the story?"

I nod.

"Umm Khalid had not yet grown used to the ache of Zayd's absence when one day soldiers surrounded her. She was standing among women, passionately sharing the words of Imam Sadiq ﷺ. She spoke of the truth of the descendants of Ali, of the Prophet's sayings, but the soldiers' spears cut her speech short. They bound her and dragged her, before the frightened eyes of the women, to the governor's palace."

I bite my lip, and Hababeh continues: "That day in the palace, many courtiers were present. Yusuf was furious, cracking sunflower seeds nervously. The soldiers forced Umm Khalid to kneel. Yusuf spat the shell of a seed toward her. He was about to speak when Umm Khalid spat in his face. Yusuf flared up, lost control, and in the blink of an eye ordered her hands to be cut off from the elbows. Do you know why?"

I shake my head 'no.' Tears well up in my eyes. I want to cry fully, not for Umm Khalid or Qanwa, but for myself. Just hours ago, before Hababeh came, before I heard the story of Sumaya, Qanwa, and Umm Khalid, I thought I had done enough standing up to oppression, defending the Imam. But now... I feel like I haven't done anything for my faith. Hababeh stays silent, a sad smile on her face, and looks at me. "Go on, Hababeh..."

Her gaze fixes on the painting of the hands, and she says, "After all, Umm Khalid's hands would shake the foundations of oppression and injustice. Those hands were her greatest treasure. With those hands, she wrote the Imam's words, and what she wrote remains for years. That means carrying the message of the Ahl al-Bayt's truth to future generations, to the people yet to come. Yusuf had Umm Khalid's hands cut off to take away her most precious gift."

"Did Umm Khalid stop narrating the hadith?"

Hababeh coughs and closes her eyelids slowly. She says, "Until her very last breath, she spoke of her Imam, of Shiism. She never wavered, not even for a moment. But after her hands were cut off, she did not live long. When Yusuf saw that cutting off Umm Khalid's hands only made her more beloved among the people, he had her beheaded to silence her voice. What he did not know was that throughout her life, Umm Khalid had trained dozens of students, and after her death, dozens of Umm Khalids lived on in Iraq."

I want to ask a question, but the door opens, and Haniya stands there. Girls carrying trays of food enter the room. I swallow my lump and move back to make space for the trays to be set down. Suddenly, a voice echoes through the hall.

"Lady Zubayda, Lady Zubayda! The Commander of the Faithful is coming to your room."

Blood rushes to my face.

A servant shouts, "He is very angry. It seems he had a long quarrel with his minister before coming here. One of the guards just brought the news."

I see fear in Haniya's eyes. At the servant's words, the girls' hands tremble. A tray slips from one of them; bowls scatter to one side; the herb dish falls to another; the roasted turkey, still on its tray, wobbles as buttermilk spills from its pitcher. My hands clench into fists. A thousand thoughts whirl in my mind. Haniya whispers, "Where should I hide this old woman, my lady?"

Voices of a veiled age

5

I wish the earth would open and swallow me whole. Swallow me, so I wouldn't have to see his eyes, hear that dragging voice, or breathe in that stench, but it's too late. He's just a few steps away from my room. I have to face him, stumble over my words, and somehow speak. Now that the spring-like fragrance of Hababeh's words has stirred my soul, now that the flood of her stories has filled my mind, now that I loathe him more than ever, how can I possibly stay calm? A gentle nudge from Haniya beside me snaps me back to reality. Her lips turn pale as a sheet.
"My lady! I've hidden Hababeh in the inner room, but if... if the Caliph pulls back this curtain, if he so much as glances that way or steps onto your balcony, we're finished."
I'd forgotten entirely about Hababeh. How could the old woman possibly hide her cough? That rasp in her chest can't be silenced. I

squeeze my eyes shut. Thoughts hammer inside my head. I square my shoulders and straighten my back. The food tray is still on the floor.

"Pick them up, Haniya."

Haniya kneels on the floor, reaching for the empty jug of yogurt, when a voice echoes through the room: "The Caliph, Commander of the Faithful, Harun al-Rashid the Great, intends to enter." Haniya lets the jug slip from her hands and rushes to stand before the door. Harun steps into the room and, with a simple wave of his hand, orders his companions to remain outside. Haniya looks straight at me. I nod. She quickly leaves and closes the door behind her. The familiar scent of Harun fills my chest, and I hold my breath. My heart tightens. A deep crimson cloak lies across his shoulders, and I can't take my eyes off the delicate gold embroidery along its edge. He steps closer, then closer still, and lifts an eyebrow.

"When you came to my chamber, your eyes were as lovely as ever, yet I failed to see them truly. Forgive me, Lady Zubayda."

It feels as if ten ragged women are trampling inside my chest. I look up as Harun moves closer. I force a smile, but his breath turns my stomach, heavy with the scent of wine, the Caliph's fine wine.

"But forgive me if I fail to see your beauty. You make no secret of your devotion to descendants of Ali, ignore our questions, and bring a guest into your private chamber, the one the guards are already whispering about. I just quarrelled with the vizier because of you. He laughed, saying that before you, I forget I am Harun. I'll show both him and you that he's wrong. Tell me, Zubayda, where is your guest? Who have you brought into my palace?"

Voices of a veiled age

Inside me, women cry out. It feels as if ten women dressed in black are throwing dust over their heads and clawing at their faces. I furrow my brows.

"Which guest? Who are you talking about? Will you ever stop with all this hostility?"

Harun's warm breath brushes against my face. His eyes are red and fevered, and he staggers slightly, then bursts into laughter.

"You sure know how to trick me. Hostile to whom? I came to see you. But it seems you've been busy. Tell me, where is she? I have nothing to do with her, believe me. I just want to see her."

My eyes harden, and I step back from him, saying, "There's no one here."

"Did you plan to eat all this food by yourself? To devour an entire lamb on your own? Let me see, there are two plates, two bowls. And this jug of syrup, did you drink it all in one go? Don't talk nonsense, Zubayda."

Harun moves toward the inner chamber. The peacock embroidered on the brown curtain dividing the room catches my eye. I run after him.

"Wait!"

"The soldiers say she does wudu like the Rafidis and prays like them. They tried to finish her off, but she disappeared. Don't tell me she was the guest of Lady Zubayda, the guest of my wife! my treacherous wife!?"

I smirk and grit my teeth.

"Do you think an old woman has come to steal your throne? You have spent years awake and restless for this, and you have spent years holding the descendants of Ali captive, afraid of losing a throne that was never yours. Don't worry, Caliph. She's not a threat to you or your throne. She's just an old woman, tired of life and its hardships. I let her into my private quarters to give her some comfort. You know I cannot turn away from someone in need, not as you would."

He lets out a wry smile, and the furrow in his brow softens. Like spring weather, he can be unpredictable, sometimes gentle and sometimes harsh. Even after all these years, I don't think I truly know him. A man who claims strength yet falters, a man of contradictions, cruel at times and merciful at others.

"Your tongue is poisonous, woman. Fine, I accept whatever you say. Just let me see that old woman. I know you could not have known she was a Rafidi. Once again, you have been softened by her helpless pleading. It is all right; I know your tender heart. But now that you know she is a Rafidi, hand her over to me. Right now."

Harun stepped forward and drew the curtain aside. I clutch his cloak. He turns back, and I meet his gaze, tears welling in my eyes. "Harun, this old woman smells like my mother. I have been starving for a mother's touch. She asks for nothing. Let her stay with me tonight, please. At first light, send your men, and I will turn her over to you. You keep me from seeing her, even though she is not my Imam. Do you remember how many times I fell at your feet, begging, 'Please… just let me stay by her side for a moment.' You didn't let me. You didn't, and the pain has stayed in my heart. This old woman is not my Imam."

Harun takes my hands in his, but I pull away. These hands are stained with blood.

"One day, Zubayda, your tearful eyes will be my undoing."

A single tear slips down my cheek.

"You are the light of my eyes, Zubayda. Without you, life holds no meaning. When you look at me, my heart stirs just as it did in my youth.

In my eyes, no one could ever be Zubayda but you. You are the beloved of this restless heart."

I grind my teeth. I remember the days when I would enter his chamber and see him staring at the dancers' waists, his gaze tracing the curves of their hips. As if he could see what was burning in my chest in my eyes, he would say, "What is it? Why don't you bare your heart and declare your love for me? Do I disgust you? Do you think Harun is deaf, blind, or dull? I am drunk, but not so far gone that I cannot see you are no longer the Zubayda you once were."

"You killed the child of Zahra, Harun, the grandson of the Prophet. I will never be the Zubayda I once was."

"Musa ibn Jafar has become your constant refrain. You speak of him always; you weep for him always. Look at me as well, Zubayda. I am your husband."

I am about to tell him, right now, that I want him no longer, that I despise him, this palace, and the Abbasid line. I am about to cry it out. My mouth opens, but he raises a threatening finger.

"By the One God, if I ever believe you have betrayed me, if I learn you plot against me, if I have allowed a traitor to hide close to me, I will cut your head from ear to ear."

I glance at the prayer beads in his hand, then at his large jewelled rings, one on his middle finger, another on his little finger, a red agate and a vivid turquoise. A fire ignites in my chest. He searches my eyes as if seeking a spark of affection, but my gaze has frozen. I offer a bitter smile. "You are not righteous, Harun. You have never been righteous... never... you..."

My lips part, struggling to find the words, but before I can speak, his hand strikes my face. The slap of his fingers against my skin echoes through the room. Henna flutters nervously, her voice shaking as she begins to chant, "Zubayda... Zubayda..."

I close my eyes as a stubborn tear slides down my cheek. Harun's voice cuts through the silence, sharp and commanding. "Truth, truth... what is truth, Zubayda? I am the truth, this palace, this wealth, this power. What do you lack, woman? If you have courage, speak. Finish your words!" He steps forward, his voice thick with anger and warning. "I slapped you so you would not think me a fool, so you would understand that even at the height of love, I can tear your head from your shoulders. At sunrise tomorrow, I will come for your guest. Woe to you if you fail to obey my command."

The sound of the door closing brings a tear rolling down my cheek. I collapse onto the bed, my face burning. The squish of Hababeh's slippers and the sharp tone of her voice as she says, "My little girl, my heart! Let me see your face, may his hand break," shatter me. My shoulders shake, and the sob I have been holding back finally bursts forth, giving voice to the chaos within me. Haniya stands in the doorway, her head hanging low, her pale face drawn with worry. "What happened all of a sudden? He was just talking about how much he loved you..."

I press my lips together, trying to hold back my sobs, but it's useless. I take a sip of the water Haniya brought and signal for her to leave the room.

"No one truly knows Harun. I've spent all these years living with a madman. Hababeh, Harun can hide a storm of rage behind the brightest smile. He can be as tender as soft wax and as cruel as a knife. He has been this way since childhood. Can you believe he spends the entire day in prayer, performing a hundred rak'ahs, and then passes the night watching fifty dancing women while drinking wine? Can you believe he weeps for the Imam all night in his prison, then collapses from grief when Fudayl 'Iyad warns him about his cruelty toward the descendants of Ali? No, no one could ever believe it. You don't understand what I mean. He's a pleasure-seeking hypocrite, a bloodthirsty man who dares to call himself a Muslim."

Hababeh nods and sits beside me. She lifts my chin gently, touching my bowed, flushed face.

"Oh, Mother, my heart aches for you."

I smile faintly.

"He wouldn't let me speak. Otherwise, I would have said everything tonight. I would have told him and every courtier that I am Shia. What could they have done? At worst, I would have shared the fate of the Abbasids and the Barmakids."

Hababeh lifts her thin brows, struggling to catch her breath as a dry cough rattles her chest. I reach out and hold her hand. She clears her throat softly and asks, "What became of the Barmakids, those who shared Harun's nights of pleasure? And Abbasah… what has become of her?"

I lace my fingers together, trying to drive the memory of Harun and his slap out of my mind. When morning comes and Hababeh leaves, I'll go to her. For now, I need to stay with this frail old woman. My thoughts reach out to Abbasah. I pull my knees to my chest and watch Hababeh in silence.

"Abbasah was Harun's sister, the one who took their mother's place. All her life, Khizran held an almost unbelievable influence over both Harun and their father. After her death, Abbasah had hoped to step into her mother's place, but my presence made that impossible. Still, she was her brother's beloved sister, and whenever sorrow shadowed Harun's heart, he would walk with Abbasah for a while, and a smile would find its way back to his face. Jafar, son of Yahya al-Barmaki, was also among Harun's closest companions. Again and again, whispers of Abbasah and Jafar's love drifted through the palace halls, yet Harun would never allow them to be together."

Hababeh moistens her dry lips and asks, "Why? What made him refuse?"

I shrug helplessly. "I don't know. Harun never showed it openly. Maybe he feared that if she married, Abbasah would drift away from him, or… honestly, I don't know, Hababeh. He never spoke of his reasons. That was just his way."

"And then? What happened after that?" she asks.

"You are even more impatient than I am."

She reaches out, her fingers lightly tracing the mark Harun has left on my face.

"Does it still hurt?"

I shake my head.

"It hurts, but not as much as my heart. Were you trying to distract me, to make my mind hold onto a story and forget the pain?"

Her gentle gaze lingers on me, and she smiles shyly.

"You faced Harun in a way I never expected. I thought you might tremble before him, or beg when he stepped toward me... yet you controlled both your words and your actions."

I rub my temple. My head feels heavy, as if it is burning. I play with my ring absentmindedly.

"Truthfully, I was shattered inside. Even now, sitting before you, my heart remains in turmoil. Yet I know how to hold myself together. I know how to smile amidst pain. I cannot say when exactly I learned it, but I did. Hababeh, do you know why I chose to stay in the palace? Years ago, I wanted nothing more than to escape."

Hababeh waves away a fly buzzing above her head. "No. Why did you change your mind, Lady?"

"Do you know Ali ibn Yaqtin? He served as Harun's minister. He invited me to stay. In name, he was the caliph's minister, but in truth, he was a devoted servant of Musa ibn Jafar؏. Once, he decided to leave the palace. He went away for a few days, then returned. I thought it was his desire for wealth and status that drew him back, but one day, in private, he told me the Imam had asked him to remain in the palace. The Imam had told him that he hoped God would work through him to heal those who had been harmed and to temper the anger of our enemies toward the saints. Hearing the Imam's words, I resolved to stay."

Hababeh asks, "Did he know you were Shia?"

"No. But Shia carry a familiar scent. It makes them trust one another, just as we trusted each other tonight. God is my witness, I never sought status or comfort. I stayed to help an orphan, to prevent injustice, but..."

A sob wells up inside me, trembling and impossible to contain. Hababeh pulls me into her embrace. "Your chest can split solid stone, yet your heart can still crack against a pebble. That is no weakness, my child. From Zubayda, the woman who drew clear water from the stubborn earth of Mecca to quench the thirst of so many, nothing less could have been born."

I pull back from her embrace, my chin quivering. "What did you just say? How do you know this story?"

Hababeh merely lifts her shoulders in a faint shrug, then reaches into the bowl, twisting a cluster of grapes free and offering it to me.

"That won't do. You haven't finished the story of Abbasah and Jafar. Tell the rest, and then I will begin mine."

I wipe my tears and pick a grape from the stem. The grape tastes sweet in my mouth, yet its aftertaste lingers with bitterness.

"Very well, I will tell you. For once, let me be the storyteller and you the listener."

"My ear is yours, my child."

I let out a long sigh. "Abbasah and Jafar had fallen in love, but no matter how many tried to intercede, Harun never gave his consent. In time, the whispers faded, yet before long, word reached us that the two had continued their secret bond, a bond that had even brought children into the world."

I press the cushion to my chest, my gaze lingering on the ivy winding up the room's central pillar. Its tendrils curl upward and cling to the stone, just as love finds its way into the hidden chambers of the heart.

"Jafar was in love, and it was that very love that destroyed him. To keep Harun distracted and blind to his affair with Abbasah, he drowned him in wine, gambling, and dancing girls. But when the truth finally reached Harun's ears, even in his drunkenness, he turned into another man. It was as if he no longer knew Abbasah or Jafar. At first, he refused to believe the whispers of his informers, but the existence of two children, hidden away in a secret house, was proof enough. You cannot imagine Harun's state of mind. His first command was that Jafar's head be severed from ear to ear. The man chosen to carry out the order trembled, hoping Harun would relent, for no one could believe he truly meant to harm Jafar, his closest confidant, the man he trusted in every great and small matter of rule. But Harun never took back his word. When Jafar's head was finally set before him on a platter, he murmured to it for a few moments in sorrow, and then ordered the executioner's head struck from his shoulders as well. He said he couldn't bear to see Jafar's killer, alive and walking before his eyes."

Hababeh bites her lip, picks a few grapes from the cluster, and places them gently in my hand.

"Harun, the man who had given the order himself…"

"Harun is a strange man, Hababeh, stranger than you can imagine. I've never met anyone like him. Nothing he does is certain; he changes from moment to moment. He is cruel, fanatical, quick to anger, and at times as stubborn as a child. From his earliest years, he was raised in the ways of nobility, surrounded by power and wealth. Yet as caliph, he must appear pious, humble, and ascetic. This duality dragged him into darkness, down to the bottom of a deep, lonely well. He was capable of deeds no one could have foreseen. In the story of Abbasah and Jafar, Harun did something that turned into a living nightmare for everyone in the palace. After Jafar was killed, he ordered the entire household destroyed. That night, the blood of the Barmakids and their servants soaked the palace floors. By dawn, Harun rose to pray. I thought the worst was over, but as the first light of morning spread across the city, he went to Abbasah's house. I stayed by his side, trying to calm him, but his anger raged like a fire that refused to die."

Hababeh starts coughing, pressing the handkerchief to her mouth, and with each cough, I see a few drops of blood bloom across the white fabric. A question flashes through my mind like lightning: "How much longer can this old woman survive in such a state?"

I place my hand on her shoulder.

"Are you feeling all right, Hababeh?"

"I'm fine, my daughter. Truly, I am. Go on."

I moisten my dry lips.

"Abbasah knelt before Harun, completely broken. She wept and pleaded, recalling their childhood games, their dreams, the sweet secrets they had once whispered to one another. But Harun watched like a marble statue. Then, as casually as if he were asking for his cup to be refilled, he gestured for the guards to step forward. They set a large chest in the middle of the room. I was speechless, unable to grasp what was unfolding before me. Four men seized Abbasah by the arms and legs. They forced her into the chest and poured her gold and clothes over her body. Can you believe that the sound of Abbasah's cries still echoes in my head? Like an echo that never fades. Her struggle, her tears, her moans, her cries, her pleas...They nailed the chest closed. Harun ordered it buried in a pit they had dug in the courtyard, then covered with bricks and lime. Do you remember what you said about Walid and the burying of women and girls alive? After all these years, Harun still

Voices of a veiled age

feels no shame in burying a living soul. Not long ago, he had his beloved sister buried alive, without a moment's hesitation."

My jaw trembles, not from longing for Abbasah or mourning Jafar, though both had played their part in my Imam's suffering.

"That day, I should have known Harun's heart was made of stone. The man who showed no mercy to his own sister, how could he ever spare Musa ibn Jafar ﷺ?

How naïve I was, how utterly foolish, to think I could ever persuade him not to be Musa ibn Jafar's ﷺ enemy!"

Hababeh stays silent. Perhaps she is thinking of that story she once heard near the end of her life, a torment so unbearable, so unthinkable, that nothing else in this world could ever compare.

I push the thought aside, lace my fingers together, and lean back against the pillow. Just let it pass, I tell myself.

"That night, I stayed with Harun until dawn, reading poetry to him, sitting by his side, and adjusting the pillow beneath his head. I thought he had finally calmed, but the next morning, just as I was spreading honey on bread for him, the door opened. His advisor entered, accompanied by two children, the sons of Abbasah and Jafar. Two fair-skinned boys with straight black hair and eyes long and beautiful, just like their mother's. Hababeh! They knew nothing, nothing of what had happened, nothing of the secret marriage, nothing at all about their parents. The morsel in my hand had gone dry. I watched Harun step forward, draw them close, and hold them so tightly I thought they might vanish into him. His hands moved over their hair and their faces. He kissed them, their eyes, their hands. My heart began to ease just a little. I thought perhaps he wanted to protect them, to shelter them beneath his wings. And then he turned, sat beside me, and took the morsel from my hand. Tears streamed down his face. With a trembling voice, he ordered the executioner to step forward and behead them. I screamed, shouted and clung to Harun. But my voice did not matter. Whatever Abbasah and Jafar had done to my Imam, their children were innocent. Completely innocent. Two little ones, eight and ten years old. My pleas were useless. The two children of Abbasah flinched like frightened sparrows, and a stream of blood ran across the room. The smell of fresh blood made me gag. Harun, Harun, staring at the blood and the severed heads, chewed his morsel with a disturbing pleasure. 'I loved these two children,' he said calmly, 'but I had to destroy them.'"

Hababeh rises, grips her cane, and walks slowly across the room, her lips moving as if whispering a prayer. I cannot make out her words, but I can feel the weight of her anguish.

"What is it, Hababeh? You seem troubled."

Her lips are pale. She stops and leans heavily on her cane.

"My Imam… in the hands of such a tyrant, one who shows no mercy to children, to his sister, or even to his friends…"

I take a deep breath and glance at Henna, sitting quietly in her cage.

"The two children were innocent, but your heart should not grieve for Abbasah and Jafar…"

Hababeh looked up at me. "Why? What crime did they commit other than love?"

"After the Imam was taken to prison, Harun, the Barmakids, and all who had cheered at his capture grew uneasy, restless, and fidgety, as if they could not quite believe it themselves. Each passing day made them more tense and worried, though they would never admit it aloud. They

were guilty of more than you think. Jafar and Abbasah paid for their cruelty to the Imam in this very world. After some time had passed since the Imam's imprisonment, Harun, the Barmakids, and all those who had rejoiced at his captivity became anxious and restless. The Imam captivated the jailers; neither curse nor complaint, neither defiance nor reproach could reach them. In prison, he stood in prayer. Sometimes he would softly ask after the jailers. If they were sad, he would calm them. If they faced a problem, he would pray for them. The jailers would not torture him, nor speak ill of him. Gradually, people's voices began to rise. Why should Musa ibn Jafar ﷺ be imprisoned? In the midst of this turmoil, Jafar and Abbasah devised a wicked, deceitful plan. Their plan was this: Harun would send his most beautiful and graceful dancer to the Imam's cell. When I first saw her, her half-bare body, her wavy hair, her painted face, and the scent of her perfume, the world spun around me. She was breathtaking, enchanting. Harun was pleased with Jafar and Abbasah's idea. The dancer he chose had captivated everyone in the palace, and they believed she could even tempt the Imam himself. Their scheme was cruel: first, she would try to shake the Imam's heart, and then she would destroy his reputation, shaming him before the people."
Hababeh, seemingly unaware of what has happened, walks back and sits beside me. I see tears in her eyes.
"Oh, Musa ibn Jafar ﷺ ..." My vision darkens. "But after a few weeks, their plan fell apart. The girl who had gone to the Imam's cell wearing a silk gown returned to the palace wrapped in coarse linen. She had become a Shia and said she had seen a man who was not of this earth. Jafar had done things like this before, Hababeh.

Harun punished him so that his punishment in the hereafter might be lighter. But who will punish Harun?"

"For now," she says quietly, "in a few hours, when the sun rises, you must hand me over to him so I can taste his punishment myself and maybe lessen my own in the hereafter."

I look into her tearful eyes and take her hand. The warmth of her thin, bony fingers strangely spreads through me.

"I will never hand you over to him. You have a great mission ahead of you. You must go to Medina, to"…

Haniya enters the room, cutting my words short. On the brass tray in her hands, a large bowl of yogurt sits beside a few pieces of bread, some salt, herbs, and water.

Still unaware of why Hababeh is here, she glances at my face, her eyebrows knitting together.

"My lady, your face is flushed… your eyes look heavy and tired. Shouldn't you rest a little?"

I glance at her small, lively figure and say, "I'm fine, Haniya. Tonight may be the best night of my life. The words of this uninvited guest, who has now become as dear to me as my own soul, have awakened me more than ever, and that is no small joy."

Haniya, not understanding a word of what I mean, stares at Hababeh in confusion.

"After you clear away the dishes and the food from the floor, go and get some rest. Come to me a few hours from now, before the call to dawn prayer. All right?"

Haniya nods and begins gathering the dishes. I move the tray closer to Hababeh and offer her the bread.

Voices of a veiled age

"It wasn't meant for you to sit at Zubayda's lavish table as a guest. Reach out, I know you haven't eaten for hours."

Hababeh says *bismillah* and steps forward.

"This bread and yogurt please me more than any feast. Did our Mawla Ali ﷻ and his children ever desire more than this? Eat now, so you'll have the strength to hear a new story. It's the story of a woman who, tonight, while listening to Harun's shouting and your firm words from behind the curtain, thought how very alike you and she are."

"I have no appetite, Hababeh. You eat. Since my Imam's martyrdom, I only take a bite when I must to stay alive."

She says nothing. I can feel Haniya's fixed gaze on us. I look at her, and she quickly comes to herself, gathers the dishes, and leaves the room. I take a small bite and let my mind drift over everything that has happened since sunset. My life has always moved quietly, calmly and without tension. Any conflicts that arose belonged to the realm of governance, to Harun. I threw myself into it willingly, so that, unlike the other women of the palace, I would not rot in idleness. I entered the world of politics hoping I might take a step for my beliefs. But this time, I am at the very heart of the storm, in the midst of the disaster itself. From sunset, from the argument with Harun, from Hababeh's arrival, from hearing scattered stories whose connection to me I still do not understand, from Harun's slap, to now, when I sit with a strange yet familiar old woman eating bread and yogurt, it all feels like a dream, sometimes a dream, sometimes a nightmare. Yet when dawn breaks, it is still me, and only me. Sometimes people sit so long on the balcony of their own house, repeating, "I am the happiest, I am the happiest," that even they start to believe it; something like repetition, habit, or perhaps self-deception. But one day, they open their eyes and realise they have been trapped in the thoughts they themselves created. Sometimes certain events lift the veil from a person's eyes, and sometimes the mind, like ploughed earth, begins to open. Then you have to sit on the balcony of your own house and face what you have spent your whole life running from, what you have feared even in shadow.

Hababeh wipes her hands and sits down beside me. I lift the tray from between us. I look at her, reclining on the pillow with her eyes closed. I imagine she has as much experience as there are lines on her face. Her presence in Harun's palace has convinced me that life, like the sea, finds its own way and brings people together.

I drink the last of the water in the glass. I reach for a thin throw to drape over her so she can take a short nap, but she sits up and rubs her eyes.

"Are you ready, my daughter?"

I slip my foot out of the slipper.

"I thought sleep had taken you with it."

She lifts her scarf from her head again, letting her fingers dance through her hair, and says, "No, I'm awake. Tonight, these stories must come to an end. I want to tell you about Siyana, a woman much like you. Siyana's gaze was full of amber, full of a light that dazzled the eyes. It was as if her eyes were filled with flowing honey, like your sweet eyes."

I smile.

"What happened, Lady Zubayda? I speak only what I see. Only you, when you smile, a dimple appears in the roundness of your face, which Siyana did not have.

She was tall and broad-shouldered, slightly full-bodied, with long, elegant fingers. Her hair was thick and lustrous, and her scent carried hints of musk, amber, and oud.

My gaze is drawn towards the incense burner. I take a deep breath, as if I can smell Siyana's fragrance. I wrinkle my nose and ask, "Was she a hairdresser?"

"Yes, the hairdresser of Pharaoh's daughter. In those days, every daughter and wife of Pharaoh had her own personal hairdresser, someone to attend to them every morning and evening, styling their hair. Siyana had been the hairdresser of Pharaoh's eldest daughter since her teenage years. She was incredibly stubborn and always full of whims. But Siyana never gave anyone a reason for complaint. She carried herself with such confidence that everyone was compelled to respect her." I let out a long yawn. Sleep presses against my eyelids, but I ask, "Of Pharaoh and his people, I only know the story of Aasiya. Who is this woman you speak of so highly?"

Hababeh presses her bony nose with the handkerchief in her hand and says, "Have you ever asked yourself what happened that made Aasiya, the Pharaoh's wife, decide to reveal her faith?"

I shake my head. Hababeh tucks the cloth into the pocket of her grey tunic and continues, "Sometimes a single word can change your life and the lives of others. Sometimes a single phrase can set your path apart from everyone else's. Siyana spoke the name of God for the first time unintentionally, but later, out of faith and from the depths of her heart, she spoke it knowingly."

In my view, Siyana's actions led Asiya to reveal her faith. Siyana was the daughter of a man who had a long-standing friendship with Khidr, a monotheist who knew and worshipped the Lord of all worlds. She had grown up in the house of a devout man and later had gone to the home of a man known in the Quran as the believer from Pharaoh's family."

The voice of the young Iranian girl reciting the verses flows through my mind, reaching the part, *"And a believing man from the family of Pharaoh who concealed his faith said, 'Will you kill a man because he says, My Lord is Allah?'"*[2] I have heard the name of the believer from Pharaoh's family many times before.

Hababeh leans forward, supporting herself with one hand, and says, "Siyana was the wife of Hezekiel. Hezekiel was Pharaoh's cousin. But Hezekiel's beliefs were worlds apart from Pharaoh's. Because he worked in Pharaoh's administration as treasurer, he held his tongue and said nothing. Sometimes you have to practice precaution; you hide your faith so that when the time is right, you can defend it and make your voice heard. Hezekiel secretly maintained contact with Moses, learning from God's prophet and listening intently to his words. Then he would pass on what he learned to Siyana. But something happened that made Hezekiel reveal his faith. After Moses' staff turned into a snake and the magicians were powerless, calling Moses a sorcerer, Pharaoh sought to have the prophet put to death. He planned a plot to kill Moses, but it was there that Hezekiel intervened. The verse goes, 'Will you kill a man for saying, My Lord is Allah, Blessed and Exalted?' After this, Pharaoh realised Hezekiel's faith and ordered him to be hanged."

I lean back against the cushion and ask, "So what happened to Siyana? Was she killed too, for being the wife of a believer?"

---

[2] Surah Ghafir Ayat 28 (40:28 Quran)

Voices of a veiled age

Hababeh coughs softly and says, "No, no one knew about Siyana's faith. Outwardly, she was no different from the other women in Pharaoh's palace. She spent time with them, laughed with them, lived among them. After Hezekiel's martyrdom, Siyana was left alone with four children who needed her. The loss of Hezekiel was a wound that never truly healed, but she had to keep her grief within the walls of her home. If she had shown too much sorrow, Pharaoh would have accused her of betrayal. Inside her home, she mourned her husband; outside, she was graceful and composed, her head held high and a steady smile on her face. She managed it well, raising her children and whispering to them about the One God, the Lord Moses had called the Creator of all worlds. As time passed after Hezekiel's death, Pharaoh grew even more arrogant, cruel, and thirsty for blood. Siyana often heard whispers here and there, rumours that after the miracle of Moses' staff and the hanging of Hezekiel, people had grown angry with Pharaoh and, deep in their hearts, had begun to turn toward Moses and his God. Those murmurs gave her comfort. She believed that no matter how much fear Pharaoh instilled in them, the people still held faith in the One God, their true Creator. One morning, like every other day, Siyana prepared to go to the palace at her usual hour. She cooked food for her sons and milked the goat, so her one-and-a-half-year-old baby would not go hungry. Hezekiel had only seen the child a few times before his death, and Siyana could not stop thinking that when her infant son grew up, he would have no memory or image of his father."

Her words remind me of the young Persian servant who used to recite the Quran with such sorrow in her voice. She once told me her father had been killed years ago in a war. She said she had never seen him, that she longed for his embrace and the warmth of his love. Just like me.

I wet my lips and twist a few strands of hair around my finger. "Siyana was right," I whisper. "That baby must have spent his whole life yearning for the father he never knew."

Hababeh stretches her legs across the bed, her eyes fixed on my hair. "No," she says softly. "Siyana's worry was in vain. That child never yearned, and he never even understood what it meant to be fatherless."

I frown. "What do you mean?"

"I'll tell you," she says. "But Zubayda, I have a question for you. You never turn away a beggar from your door, and you treat your servants like your own daughters. Is there a reason for that? I think perhaps losing your father so young, knowing the pain of being an orphan, has made you this way. Or maybe it's because your mother was once a servant herself, and that's why you feel such compassion for the poor. Am I right?"

I want to pour out everything I've kept buried, the sorrow that's lingered since I first heard the story of my mother's life in servitude, the ache of loneliness that has taken root in me since my father's death. I want to speak the unspeakable, but something strange holds my tongue still, sealing the words inside me.

I smile faintly and whisper, "I don't have an answer to that. Will you tell me more about Siyana?"

Hababeh nods and says softly, "You're right. I must tell you about Siyana. Time is short. That day, Siyana prepared her baby's milk, entrusted him to his older brothers, and left the house. Pharaoh's daughter had sent a carriage for her, but Siyana ignored it and chose to walk to the palace. The comb she had run through her hair shimmered in the sunlight, catching the eyes of many who saw her. The palace guards stepped aside to let her pass, and she made her way toward the smaller palace that belonged to Pharaoh's daughter. The courtyard was full of life, blooming with red and yellow flowers, alive with the songs of birds and the gentle murmur of flowing water. Siyana plucked a flower from the garden to adorn the princess's hair. She saw the princess sitting beneath a tree at the far end of the courtyard, resting on her ornate chair while a woman nearby played the lute for her. Siyana stepped forward. When the princess saw her, her face lit up with delight. With a flick of her hand, she dismissed the musician and then lifted her chin proudly. 'Today I want you to style my hair so that I'll be the most beautiful woman in the palace,' she said. 'Let me see that comb you used on your hair; it shines so beautifully.' Siyana, who held little affection for Pharaoh's household, forced a polite smile. Memories from long ago stirred within her, of the day when Moses's sister had come to her, eyes red from crying, her face drawn with worry. Siyana had tried again and again to learn what had happened, but the girl had said nothing. A few days later, she returned in despair, and this time her heart opened like a ripe pomegranate. She told Siyana that her mother had set their infant son afloat on the Nile and that the baby was now in Aasiya's care, crying endlessly for his mother's milk. The princess's voice pulled Siyana back to the present. She was only a few years younger than Siyana, though she carried herself like a grown woman, and she gestured for Siyana to step closer.

Siyana stepped closer to the princess's chair and remembered the day she had reassured Moses's sister. She had hurried to Aasiya, taken the crying infant in her arms, and promised a solution for his endless tears, pointing out Moses's sister to Aasiya. That day, Aasiya had clung to Moses's sister as if she had discovered a ruby in the midst of a desert, begging her to fetch the boy's mother. But Moses's sister had frowned, saying that allowing commoners and the poor to enter the home of someone like Pharaoh would diminish the dignity of God and His house. Siyana pushed these thoughts aside and bowed slightly to the princess. She reached for the comb in her hair while the princess also extended her hand. Siyana gritted her teeth and took the comb into her own hands. A few strands of hair were tangled between its teeth. The girl pulled on the comb, but the strands refused to come loose. She twisted her neck, saying, "Your hair is wrapped around this comb like a rope," and then she let it go. The comb slipped from her hands and fell to the ground."

I rest my hand under my chin and stare at Hababeh. Before my eyes, I see Pharaoh's garden: red, yellow, and pink flowers, large fountains, birds hopping from branch to branch and singing, and a sprawling tree casting its shade over a single chair. On the chair, a girl crouches, dressed in a gown encrusted with stones and pearls, her black hair twisted into curls, her nose slightly upturned, her lips small. Behind her stands a short woman, gently fanning her with a peacock-feather fan. I see Siyana, a woman much like myself, and the glint of the golden comb lying on the ground. But is the falling of a comb really such a significant event?

I hug my knees and ask, "Hababeh, you talk about the comb falling as if Siyana had stood before Pharaoh and spat in his face. It's just a comb." She laughs, soft and gentle like the spring rain.

"What are you saying, my dear? Surely the falling of a comb holds a secret, or I wouldn't tell it this way."

I lift the candleholder Haniya had lit before leaving and hold it near Hababeh's face. The light of twelve candles falls across the wrinkles of her face.

"I must have tired you with all these questions. Honestly, the night is far gone, and in this silence, sleep swirls around me more than anything else. But you, as if you've seen the dawn, you burn with energy and speak. Your strength is truly remarkable."

She moistens her lips, her dark, bead-like eyes sparkling. "These stories weigh heavily on my heart, and you are a good listener. You are worthy of this secret, and I am glad to spend the last days of my life beside you."

"You're coming here tonight, just as I still wear my mourning clothes for my Imam, in these days when the grief of his departure still presses on my chest, it feels like a miracle. Had I not spoken with you, sorrow would have consumed me, and I might have died in it."

"You are stronger than you think, Zubayda. Now, let me continue the story. There is little time before dawn, and I still have more to tell."

I nod and lend her my ear, ready to listen as she begins.

"When the comb fell, Siyana's gaze shifted between the Pharaoh's daughter and the comb. She bent down to pick it up, but suddenly a sharp pain shot through her back. She had just given birth, and after her husband's death, she hadn't been taking proper care of herself. As the pain bit into her, her lips moved involuntarily. 'Oh God...' she murmured, and that single word eased Siyana's pain but made the Pharaoh's daughter's ears prick up. She glanced at Siyana and pursed her lips. Siyana stood behind her. She pulled a wooden comb from the daughter's special box and began to comb her hair. Then she divided it into two sections and started braiding. She braided one section and tied the end with a golden ribbon. Then she began braiding the second section, and the Pharaoh's daughter asked softly, 'Tell me, is the God you mentioned when you picked up the comb the same as my father? I mean… did you mean my father?'"

"What did Siyana say?"

"The truth," she said. "She said no. She meant the One God, the only God, who is yours and mine, and your father's too."

I wave my hands in the air. "But why? Why did she do that? A single yes could have saved her. She had children at home, a newborn still nursing."

Hababeh shakes her head slowly. "At first, even the Pharaoh's daughter didn't understand what she'd heard. But when she saw the brightness in Siyana's eyes and the proud lift of her chest, she realised it. After Hezekiel's martyrdom, Siyana had seen with her own eyes, in the narrow alleys of the city and in the halls of the palace, how deeply people had come to love Moses and the God of Moses. She saw that the blood of an innocent had awakened many hearts, and she was certain the time for hiding was over. She had to do something for the God she had always worshipped and believed in. Pharaoh was not God, and Siyana wanted to show that."

I shake my head. "What are you saying, Hababeh? If they imprisoned her, what would happen to her children? Didn't her nursing baby need his mother?"

A sorrowful smile touches Hababeh's lips. She coughs softly, then stares down at her hands.

Voices of a veiled age

"A few moments before he was hanged, Hezekiel had whispered something in Siyana's ear that warmed her heart. He had said he was entrusting Siyana and her children to the same God who could save a tiny infant from the rushing waters of the Nile, bring him to Pharaoh's palace, and turn him into the voice of God before Pharaoh's mighty throne. Hezekiel had said that such a God would surely protect Siyana and her children. Now Siyana, too, had decided to entrust her children to the God of Moses."

I draw my knees close and ask, "So Hezekiel never loved Siyana? Or did Siyana never love her children?"

Hababeh runs a hand over her mole and says, "Stop clinging to those tangled fairy-tale ideas people call love, my dear. What is love to you? A chain around your feet? If that's what you believe, then you've already missed the chance to love. Love should give you wings to fly. The constant aches, the open and unhealed wounds, those are not love. Love is a gift from God, a longing He places in His servants so they may find their way to the heavens, to the joy of true love. Sometimes letting go and walking away is the proof of loving the One who is truly worthy of love."

She speaks the truth. I have never tasted earthly love. Hababeh is right. My love for Harun was like a mirage.

Hababeh fixes her gaze on a candle flame that has melted faster than the rest and says:

"The daughter of Pharaoh was frozen. She kept repeating Siyana's words to herself, one God, the One and Only. Then, for a moment, it felt as if something had exploded inside her. She leapt from the seat. With her hair half-braided, she ran without pause. She ran toward

Pharaoh's court and, along the way, shouted, 'That woman, seize that woman. She follows Moses.' The comb slipped from Siyana's hands, and her tongue stuck to the roof of her mouth. She widened her eyes to see if the guards were coming, but there was no sign of them. Only Pharaoh's daughter's maid watched her with her mouth half-open. Siyana threw the comb onto the chest and tried to rush out of the palace to reach her children. But the sound of the soldiers' boots stopped her. The soldiers formed a circle around her, and Pharaoh stepped forward. The girl, with the same half-braided hair, pointed at Siyana and shouted, 'Father! She said she does not accept you as a god, and that her God is the One and Only.'

Women are strange creatures. Sometimes they are infinitely merciful, and other times utterly cruel. How is it that women forget God created them from the same flesh? Did Pharaoh's daughter not spare a single thought for Siyana? To her fragile, feminine heart, to the motherly breasts that had given milk, to the dim eyes of one who had just lost her first love?"

Hababeh casts a glance at me.

"When Pharaoh took his seat, they brought Siyana before him with her hands bound. Pharaoh smirked and said, 'Lift your head.' And Siyana stared into his eyes. Soldiers stood all around, and the men and women of the palace had come to watch. Asiya was there too, her face full of worry. Pharaoh shouted, 'Say that I am your god and go home without a word.' But Siyana moistened her dry lips and replied firmly, 'My God is the One and Only. The God of all. My God, you, and Moses.' Pharaoh's clenched teeth made Siyana's heart tremble, but she did not lose herself. Inside, she was crumbling, just like you would, yet she still managed to keep her composure."

I smile, but the bitterness of it brings a lump to my throat. All this pretending to be strong has torn the fabric of my being apart, and now I feel as if my heart has shattered into a thousand pieces.

"Wasn't Siyana afraid?" I ask.

Hababeh rubs her knees, lets out a weary sigh, and says, "Faith is stronger than fear. Don't you ever feel afraid? Yet your faith keeps you standing. Siyana, too, believed that God's gaze was with her. The sun beat down on the palace courtyard. Pharaoh had found a new amusement. Ignoring Aasiya's pleas to calm himself, he drank goblet after goblet of wine. Then came the sound of crying. Siyana turned and saw her sons in the courtyard, hands bound, eyes wet. Even her nursing infant, restless in the arms of a guard, squirmed and kicked."

I pull myself forward. "Was Siyana alone? Didn't anyone support her? To stand by her…"

"My daughter! Love, faith, and death are three experiences a person must face alone. That day was the day Siyana's faith was tested, and she had to show on her own that deep in her heart she believed in the One God. Faith goes beyond words. A person's belief must be reflected in action. Siyana's sons gathered around her, and her hands were freed so she could hold her infant. Pharaoh said nothing, and the people of the palace watched every move of his lips. As soon as Siyana calmed her baby, Pharaoh smiled and gestured for a guard to come forward. He whispered something into the guard's ear that no one heard. Then he shouted, 'I wish there were a musician here to play for us! Today is a day of joy.'"

Pharaoh reminds me of Harun; days pass, life moves on, and people repeat themselves. It is as if every newborn who opens their eyes steps into the place of someone who came before. Whose steps have I taken? I lift my eyebrows and fill my chest with air. The drum and lute sound the warning that Siyana's heart will be torn apart. Harun is another Pharaoh, and I have seen these deeds from him.

Hababeh takes my hand. "Yes, the line of Pharaohs still continues. That day, besides the drum and lute, Pharaoh wanted something else: a large cauldron full of molten copper. The guards kindled a fire and set the cauldron on top. The flames leapt up, the people whispered among themselves, Siyana's children wept silently, the lute player played, and the copper began to boil."

I blink rapidly, rubbing my eyes, but it does no good. Hababeh drags her thumb across my hand.

"When the copper began to boil, rivulets spilled from the cauldron onto the ground. Steam rose, and its sharp scent filled the air. Pharaoh smiled and turned to his daughter. 'Which one do you think we should place in the cauldron first? After all, you recognised the traitors, and this is your reward.' The girl approached Siyana. Slowly, deliberately, she displayed her half-braided hair to the crowd and said, 'This woman has served me faithfully until today. Now I will repay her service and let her choose the first victim herself. Siyana, which of your sons would you like to see melted first, hmm?' Tears brimmed in Siyana's eyes and spilled down her cheeks. Pharaoh's daughter pointed at the eldest son and continued, 'I think this one will do. He reminds me of Hezekiel. Perhaps it will bring him to mind for you.' At her words, a guard grabbed the boy by his shirt and dragged him across the ground. The

Voices of a veiled age

boy screamed, clawing at the floor. He ran to his mother, throwing his arms around her. His brothers began to sob, the spectators held their breath, and Siyana wailed. The boy begged, 'Mother, save me.' Siyana pulled her son to her chest, trying to calm him, when Pharaoh shouted, 'Say that by 'God' you mean me. Then take your children's hands and go home.' Zubayda! That moment was unbearable for Siyana. She saw the devil everywhere, heard his voice in every corner of the garden, urging her to speak and comply with Pharaoh's demand. Her son was grown, and seeing his death would destroy her."

Another candle goes out. I hold a bowl of water toward Hababeh. Siyana! How could you choose? You are my guiding light, my mentor. How did you prove your faith?

Hababeh clears her throat and continues, "Siyana decided to say that by 'God' she meant Pharaoh. She could not bear the death of her child. She raised her hand to stop Pharaoh, but suddenly she remembered her husband's words, the ones he always said: 'People believe there is no power greater than Pharaoh's, so they think he is their god and creator. We must shatter this idea.' Siyana swallowed her words, whispered the name of Moses' God, and the devils drew back, farther away. Siyana's silence angered Pharaoh. With the press of Pharaoh's eyelid, a guard thrust Siyana's son into the cauldron. At first, only his head was above the molten copper, and Siyana saw his eyes wide with terror. Then his head sank beneath the surface, leaving only his hands, flailing in the air, reaching for help, before the cauldron swallowed him completely."

I pull my hand from Hababeh's. Cold washes over me again. The chill runs through my bones. I hug my arms to myself. I remember the day Harun discovered that one of his advisors was a Shiite. He summoned him, and after a few minutes, the executioner was called. A leather mat was spread at Harun's feet. First the hands, then the feet, and finally the head, severed at Harun's command. I had closed my eyes, but a slimy wetness splashed across my face. The red blood of Ali's ؑ devoted follower had formed a thin stream, its droplets striking my cheeks. This sudden, severe punishment was a delight for Pharaoh and for Harun as well.

Hababeh continues in a trembling voice.

"This happened three times. Siyana's three eldest sons burned before her eyes in Pharaoh's fire. Siyana thought she had gone mute. She had clawed at the ground so fiercely that blood ran under her nails. She had pulled her hair and thrown dust over her head so much that everyone thought she would collapse completely. At Pharaoh's signal, they pulled the infant from Siyana's arms. She held him to her chest like a precious gem, but the sharp tip of a guard's spear pressing into her side forced her to loosen her grip. The infant was placed in Pharaoh's arms. He kissed the baby's forehead and whispered, 'Siyana! You and your disloyal husband have served in my palace and for me. I want to give you another chance. Say that you do not recognise Moses' God and that I am your Lord. Then you can take your baby in your arms and go home.' Siyana lifted her gaze from the infant in Pharaoh's arms and fixed it on the cauldron, its steam rising to the sky. Her chin trembled. Asiya tried to step forward to speak, but Pharaoh's piercing gaze forbade it. Pharaoh's daughter, however, tossed her head and said, 'Father, have no mercy on her. Mercy among these people leads only to chaos. You should have severed their heads the day you hanged her husband. Then she would not have dared to say with such certainty that her God is Moses' God.

Voices of a veiled age

You were not there and did not see how she looked at me with scorn and said that you are not God and all of this is a lie.' Pharaoh's anger flared again. He pressed the infant to his chest, and the baby's cries rang out. A soldier took the infant from Pharaoh's hands, and Siyana's heart pounded wildly in her chest."

In the dim and flickering light of the room, I press my head against the wall and stare at the ceiling. Its patterns blur before my eyes. I look at Hababeh in silence. She coughs and takes a sip of water. I say nothing. There is nothing to say. Hababeh is right. Faith is stronger than fear. Siyana was a mother. With each child's death, her heart was torn, her soul shattered, and her life seemed to leave her body. Yet she held herself together, only and entirely because of her faith, to prove that the One God is the God of all. Seeing that I have no strength left, Hababeh continues. This time, she is lying on her side at the corner of the bed, her robe draped over her legs.

"A heart can tremble for a single moment, but that one moment can change your destiny. If the heart trembles for God, nothing but safety awaits. But if it trembles for anyone else, you must expect a storm, a fierce storm. That day, Siyana never took her eyes off Pharaoh's lips. She reached for her infant in the soldier's arms, pressed him to her chest, inhaled his scent, and a tear fell from her eye onto the baby's cheek. She wanted to press a kiss to his red face and soothe his restless cries with milk when she saw the baby's lips moving. Can you believe it? A soft voice came from the infant. Siyana doubted her ears, but the silence of the crowd and Pharaoh, half-risen and staring wide-eyed at the child, forced her to believe what she heard. The infant had opened his mouth from inside the swaddle and said, 'Mother! Why do you fear? The One God is with us...'"

I rise to my feet, unable to believe it. "What are you saying, Hababeh? Wasn't speaking in childhood supposed to be the miracle of Jesus, son of Mary?" Hababeh smiles, the candlelight softening her eyes.

"Yes. But this miracle has not happened only once in history. Whenever the sigh of the oppressed rises to the heavens, whenever someone suffers for their faith, God becomes their comfort. Sometimes a newborn's voice becomes God's voice. Once in the story of Jesus, once to prove the purity and chastity of Prophet Joseph, once to lift the sorrow from Khadijah the Great. Siyana's infant had come to make her heart tremble for God and to reveal to all the emptiness of Pharaoh's claim to divinity."

I stand beside Henna's cage, leaning against the wall. The sweet scent of musk from the shelves fills my nose. Now I am in the darkness, and Hababeh sits in the light.

"Hearing the infant's voice pierced through Siyana's fear like an arrow of light cutting through the night and settled in her heart. She kissed her child's mouth, lifted her head, and shouted with a strong voice, 'My God is the God of all of you. The One who created me, the One who is unparalleled, the One who gave a newborn the ability to speak...' Murmurs rose from the crowd, everyone had an opinion, and Pharaoh grew uneasy. He feared that a newborn could challenge his claim to divinity more than anyone else. And indeed, the people's ears and eyes were alert, each speaking their thoughts. Suddenly, from the crowd, a voice rang out, 'I believe in the God who can give a newborn the power to speak.' Hearing that voice, Pharaoh stood. They pulled the infant from Siyana's arms, and a guard threw him, still swaddled, into the cauldron. He sank into the molten copper and did not come out. At Pharaoh's signal, the soldiers turned to Siyana. She neither cried nor struggled. She pushed their hands away and walked toward the cauldron herself. The guards fed the fire beneath the cauldron, and the heat hit Siyana's face. She looked at Pharaoh and said, 'Pour what remains of my children and me into the courtyard of our home.' Pharaoh, unable to believe that anyone could make such a request in the face of death, simply nodded. With a heart-wrenching cry, Siyana surrendered her body to the molten copper, and her voice fell silent. But her silence became the spark for countless other voices, all proclaiming faith in the God of Moses."

It is good that Hababeh cannot see my face, my withered expression, or the redness of my eyes from crying.

"What suffering, what unbearable torment! I could not have imagined a torture like this."

Hababeh slowly comes toward me, takes my hand, and I melt into her embrace. She whispers into my ear, "Hardships are like the wind. Wind has no roots. It does not stay. But a person's faith and heart are not like the wind. They are not like an inn. An inn hosts a caravan each day. A caravan stops for a while and moves on another day. Have you ever seen inns? What am I saying… You yourself have an inn, many inns."

She knows how to make my imagination soar from one place to another. I see her eyes in the flickering light of the room, and I want to emerge like a sprout from the soil. Hababeh squeezes my hand and says, "Tell me about the inns. Tell me about the Qur'an whose rubies you removed, leaving empty spaces. Tell me about the spring of Zubayda…"

Voices of a veiled age

I run my hand over the Qur'an on the shelf. The image of Siyana and the cauldron full of molten copper is burned behind my eyelids.

Voices of a veiled age

6

"I drew back the curtain of the palanquin,[3] and my world shattered. I had never imagined my heart could break like fragile glass at the sight of them, standing under the scorching sun. Yet it happened, sooner than I thought. Before my mind could argue, the mothers had sent the girls on purpose; my heart told me they had no other choice. Each girl held a bowl in her hands. The sun showed no mercy on their delicate skin. They stood, sunburned and dishevelled, before the palanquin, and the youngest among them, in a long crimson dress that dragged on the ground, was crying. Tears fell onto the dust, and it felt as if my own heart bled. Their lips were cracked and dry. I did not need to kneel to hear

---

[3] A covered litter or portable carriage, often richly decorated, carried on the shoulders of bearers. In many historical cultures, including the Islamic and Persianate worlds, it was used to transport nobles, royalty, or women of high status in privacy and comfort.

their plea. Those lips, those dirt-streaked hands, the bowls held high, they all cried together: 'Water, Water.' In their tearful eyes, I saw a three-year-old child, parched and desperate. The word 'water' brought the noonday of Ashura vividly back to life in my mind."

I rubbed my eyes and looked at Hababeh. She sat at the edge of the bed, staring at the floor. I, however, could not stay still. Once, twice, three times, I paced the length of the room.

"Now that I think back, I realise that years ago, before I had fallen in love with Harun, I promised myself never to forget my own heart, my goals, my beliefs. I promised to stay true to them, never letting being a wife or mother define me completely. I promised not to let life destroy me from within. I promised to fight for my desires, to win. But I forgot those promises. That day, when I looked into the eyes of the little girls from Mecca begging for water, I remembered who I was, for a brief moment. The Zubayda inside me, older now and streaked with grey, commanded the palanquin to stop. The soldier hesitated, worried that I was stopping without Harun's permission, but I ignored him. I stepped down, and the sun's rays embraced me. People surrounded me: young women, ashamed men, and wrinkled, desperate elders. They wailed against the drought that had seized their land, slowly driving their lives toward ruin."

Hababeh's voice was quiet, hoarse. "What did Harun say? Did he stop and listen to the people?"

I sneer and sigh, "He stopped, but he did not get down. He sent his vizier to find out what was happening, then sent word that I should mount and move on. He said there was nothing he could do for the people and that I must remember we had come for the pilgrimage, not to bring aid to a people with endless needs."

"And you?" she asked.

I smile, still feeling a rush of joy and satisfaction at the memory, "I did not back down," I say. "That day, I was completely myself. I told the vizier to tell Harun to go to the caravanserai[4] and wait while I handled the matter. The vizier left and never returned. Harun's palanquin stayed where it was. I turned to an old man standing beside me, his eyes shifting between Harun and me, and said, 'I know of your struggle, but what is the solution? Rain is God`s work, a blessing. Neither I nor anyone else can command the clouds to pour over the people of Mecca and fill their rivers.' The old man leaned on his cane and, rising above the murmur of the crowd, said, 'We must pray to God for rain, but you might be able to help untangle this problem. There is a region nearby with abundant qanats[5] and flowing springs. Every few days, we fetch water from there so our women and children do not die of thirst. But this is not a sustainable way to live. The mother's milk has run dry from thirst; the children's skin and hair have become ill. We need water for

---

[4] A roadside inn built along major trade routes—especially across the Middle East, Persia, and Central Asia—where travelling caravans could rest, resupply, and find shelter. Caravanserais typically enclosed a central courtyard and served as vital hubs for commerce, culture, and safe passage along long desert and Silk Road journeys.

[5] An ancient underground water-channel system developed in Persia and used across the Middle East. Qanats tap groundwater from a distant source—often in higher terrain—and guide it through gently sloping tunnels to supply towns, fields, and settlements with a steady flow of fresh water. This ingenious engineering allowed communities to thrive in arid regions long before modern irrigation.

drinking, washing, ritual purification, bathing, and a thousand other daily needs.'"

Hababeh hugged the pillow. "Then why didn't they divert a river from there to their region?" she asked.

Henna had buried her head between her wings and dozed off. I looked at her, then lifted the Qur'an wrapped in silk from the shelf. I drew back the silk and ran my hand over its leather cover.

"I thought it might be possible too, but that region was far from Mecca, farther than I had imagined. The old man, noticing me deep in thought and eager to help, beckoned a young man. 'Explain to Lady Zubayda how this drought can be solved,' he said. As the young man spoke, I realised it was possible to channel a spring from Hunayn to Mecca, but it would demand great expense. The dry, unyielding soil around Mecca resisted every strike of shovel and pickaxe. It would take hours of toil and sweat just to break the earth. All I wanted was to ease their troubles, to see even the faintest spark of hope in their eyes. So, I said, 'Even if every strike of the pickaxe costs a dinar, I want the work done. I want water to reach Mecca.' The architects began to lay out their plan, but all I could see were the people's cheers, the bright faces of children bouncing with joy in their mothers' arms. When Harun heard the clamour, he came down. A soldier held a canopy over his head, and the moment he appeared, the crowd fell silent. He swept his gaze over them, then leaned close and whispered in my ear, 'You can count on my help.'"

The memory of Harun's behaviour still unsettles me. How did I not turn away from him that very day? I walked toward the bed. Hababeh leaned back as I crouched before her, holding the Qur'an tight against my chest. She scratched the tip of her nose; from the way her eyes lingered, I knew she longed to see the Holy book. But instead, she said, "I see. So Harun agreed to help you."

I shrugged lightly.

"He has a habit of stepping forward wherever there's applause, a reward to be claimed, or a chance for his name to be spoken. Let me tell you a sweeter story. Years ago, one evening, I had gone out of the palace with Haniya for a walk. As dusk fell, I turned back toward the palace, with Henna at my side. Near the gates, I saw Buhlul sitting on the ground, playing with flowers. Buhlul was no child; he was a grown man, yet simple-hearted. Harun believed him mad, but to me, he was neither a fool nor insane. His mind and reasoning, I always thought, worked more soundly than most. I stepped closer. Henna's voice called behind me, "Zubayda, Zubayda," again and again, but Buhlul did not turn. I stood over him and saw what he was making: with bits of flowers and stems, he had shaped a small garden, planting a stalk of wheat among a few petals. 'What are you doing, Buhlul?' I asked. 'I am building paradise,' he said. 'And will you sell me this paradise?' I asked. Without hesitation, he replied, 'Yes, for one hundred dinars.' I told Haniya to give him the money. He tossed the purse into the air and laughed. 'I'll send you the deed, sealed and stamped,' he said. I looked at his worn clothes and shook my head, yet I was content to see him smile. Later, back at the palace, I told Harun the story. His face darkened. He said I should never trust that madman."

My gaze drifted to the extinguished candles in the candelabrum. They melted faster than the others, as if they burned with greater heat, or perhaps burning pleased them deeper than shining light.

"What happened, Zubayda? You are not telling the end," Hababeh said.

I started, my thoughts no longer fully in my control.

"I was not well that night. When I finally closed my eyes, I dreamed I was in paradise. Houris[6] gathered around me, and before me lay a garden, just like the one Buhlul had made from flowers. At dawn, I told Harun about my dream. Eager to claim that paradise for himself, he summoned Buhlul to the palace. Buhlul came quietly and sat without a word. Harun asked him to build a paradise he could buy, but Buhlul ignored him. Harun offered a thousand dinars instead of a hundred, but Buhlul only shook his head. 'No, Lady Zubayda, my paradise cannot be bought with money alone. You, however, saw its fruits, and from that your generosity flowed.' Then he rose and walked away. I followed him and found that he had given the hundred dinars, in my name, to the less fortunate in the city.'"

I cannot help but laugh, recalling Buhlul's calm face and Harun's flushed one, his jealousy over me and my little paradise. I couldn't help but laugh again. Hababeh took my hand.

"My dear! You're smiling again, and that dimple is back on your cheek. Both Buhlul and Harun are strange, extraordinary, almost legendary. So, on that day in Mecca, did you accept Harun's help?"

My smile faded. In my mind, I was back in Mecca, beside the palanquin, among the sunburned girls. "Outwardly, yes. But I had promised myself I would not take a single dinar from him. And I kept that promise. I

---

[6] Houris (Ḥūr al-'Ayn): According to Shia Islamic tradition, the Houris are pure, luminous beings created by Allah as companions for the righteous in Paradise. Described in the Qur'an as immaculate and free from all human flaws, they symbolise the spiritual rewards, tranquillity, and divine beauty of the Hereafter.

sold every jewel I owned, gave all my savings, even the precious stones from this Qur'an."

I held out the Qur'an to Hababeh. The empty settings where the stones had once gleamed were still visible. She took it in her hands and pressed a kiss to its cover, and whispered, "Because of your generosity, water flowed to the people of Mecca. And in gratitude, they named it Zubayda's Well. I know well, Lady Zubayda, that this was far from your only act of kindness. Years later, when you returned for Hajj, the people once again turned to you in need. You ordered the well of Zamzam to be deepened to ease the water shortage. You saw how so many had no proper shelter, how endless streams of pilgrims had to spend the night under the scattered trees along the road. So, you ordered grand caravanserais to be built, both in the city and along the long road, giving weary travellers a safe place to rest. You knew well that charity is like an ancient tree, its blessings bearing fruit through the ages."

Had I heard these words from Hababeh at any other time, they would have filled me with a warmth beyond words. But now, I feel nothing but heaviness. I slide my ring off my finger, then slip it back on again. "I feel as if somewhere along the way, I've lost my path. I've wandered so far down the wrong road that I no longer have the strength to turn back."

Her voice drifts softly across the quiet room. "Zubayda, my moonlit lady, every human being has the right to grow weary, to feel lost or confused, to forget their path, to stumble in despair, to sink into stillness, even to feel cold and spiritless. And what is wrong with that? You will remain in this state only briefly. Very soon, you'll realise there is no miracle greater than life itself, and you will come alive again.

Zubayda, the sun always rises after the darkest night. I think sometimes a person must see everything as lost, sometimes feel the shadow of defeat beside their own shadow. But at some point, one breaks through the fences, makes a new choice, and rises above the clouds. So give yourself a chance."

I hug my knees and watch her. The corner of my eye twitches again.

"Hababeh, I was wrong. I should have ended Harun back then."

Hababeh looks at me with unfocused eyes. "What are you saying, child?"

I shrug, my voice rough. "A little poison in his food would have been enough. I had access to his wine, his dish, his tray of sugared almonds."

"God forbid, child. What kind of thoughts have gripped you?"

"These are not new thoughts. I've carried them for a long time. If I had killed Harun, my Imam ﷺ would still be alive, Hababeh."

Hababeh furrows her brows. "Killing someone, with poison and in secret, is not the way of the lovers of the Ahl al-Bayt."

My chin trembles. The twitch in my eye wouldn't stop. "That is what kept me from doing it. That is what made me sit and watch the martyrdom of Musa ibn Ja'far ﷺ. If you had been in my place, what would you have done?"

Hababeh begins to cough, dry and harsh. I take the Qur'an from her hand. She folds her handkerchief and presses it to her mouth. I fill her bowl with water. She drank, then whispered, "Are you ready to hear the last story? We do not have much time."

I nod and place the Qur'an on its stand at the corner of the bed. The thought of her leaving washes over me. I blink and lean closer to listen.

Voices of a veiled age

"The redness of your eyes shows how much strength you've lost. Even Henna, restless since dusk, has fallen asleep. I know tonight has been hard for you, but I do not expect to see you again in this world."

I pulled myself forward on the bed. I hold Hababeh against my chest and whisper, "Life has been harsh and breathless for a long time. When the sun set and Harun called me to his room, I decided to face him. The words I am a Shia rose to the tip of my tongue, but his furious shouting silenced me. I left Harun's room distraught, and then Haniya told me how much you insisted on seeing me. At first glance, I felt you were familiar. As time passed, your kindness sank deeper into my heart. When you spoke, I understood it was love for the descendants of Ali ﷺ that had brought you, that you had come to be my companion. To tell the truth, Hababeh, your sudden arrival was like a storm. Now I'll face Harun with more certainty than ever, perhaps tomorrow morning, as soon as you leave. I am so glad you came, Hababeh."

She slips out of the circle of my arms. Her eyes are laughing, her lips too. Her sweet smile shows her contentment. She says, "Come, rest your head in my lap; this is the last tale. I want to braid your hair and tell you about a woman in whom motherhood overflowed."

A strange lump tightens in my throat. I rest my head on Hababeh's lap, curling in on myself as her fingers gently comb through my long hair. My eyelids close, and a single tear falls on her skirt.

"It was a wedding, a magnificent wedding unlike any you have seen. Unlike your wedding with Harun, no jewels or emeralds, no chests of gold, no gowns of silk or brocade. The guests came from the heavens.

Voices of a veiled age

Our Prophet ﷺ led the way, angels followed, chanting with joy. The bride was Fatima ؑ, the light of the Prophet's eye, and the groom was Ali ؑ, his brother and successor.

When they brought the bride home, the Prophet ﷺ placed Fatima's ؑ hand in Ali's. He saw her cheeks flush with colour and Ali's ؑ lips pale with modesty, and he smiled, praying for them. He left reassured, leaving Fatima ؑ in peace, confident that though she had no mother, Barakah would pour over her the most genuine care of a mother's love."

"Barakah," Hababeh murmurs, "what a beautiful, musical name!"

In a murmur, Hababeh says, "That night, Barakah wept with joy; she circled Fatima ؑ, scattering incense. With the help of the Prophet's ﷺ companions, she had prepared Fatima's ؑ trousseau, set her home in order, worn the bridal gown herself, and then given it to the poor. She read the secrets of Ali ؑ and Fatima's ؑ hearts in their eyes and pleaded for the wedding to be hastened. She was not Fatima's ؑ mother, yet she would have given her life for her."

I tilt my head and ask, "Fortunate Barakah. Was she called that because her name sounded so beautiful?"

Hababeh smiles, her fingers gently combing through my hair. "No. She was a dark-skinned woman with black eyes, thick lashes, and fine lines beneath her lids. Have you heard the story of Abraha's army, the one that marched with elephants to destroy the Kaaba?"

"I have," I reply. "My grandfather told me the tale of the elephants and the ababeel [7], over and over again."

---

[7] Mentioned in the Qur'an (Surah al-Fīl), the Ababeel are flocks of birds sent by God to destroy the army of Abraha as it marched toward the Kaaba. According to Islamic

Voices of a veiled age

Hababeh fusses with my hair. "When Abraha's army marched toward Mecca, young Barakah was with her family among them. Abraha came planning to settle, but he was defeated, and Barakah was taken captive along with the soldiers. Yet that captivity was sweeter to her than any freedom could ever be. The Prophet's ﷺ grandfather took her under his wing. Seeing her innocence, he made her both servant and companion to Aaminah, the Prophet's ﷺ mother. After Aminah's husband died, she was left lonely, and the Prophet's ﷺ grandfather understood. Barakah became Aminah's confidante, the one who bore her sorrows. In Aminah's care, in a place of respect and dignity, she grew to maturity, cared for him like a second mother. When Aminah passed away, Muhammad ﷺ became Barakah's whole world. From the time he was six until he married Khadijah, she served in the Prophet's household."

I lift my head from her lap. "Why tell me Barakah's story? She was wrapped in the Prophet's kindness all her life…"

She smiles. The candles have melted away; only an oil lamp still burns. Hababeh raises the flame. "The Age of Ignorance is only a word, but living in it and standing against it is not for everyone. When the Prophet first declared himself God's messenger and called people to abandon idolatry, no one stood with him, but Barakah did. She was the fourth person to believe in the Prophet ﷺ. Faith is not easy, Zubayda. A belief you must stand by and defend with your life, especially among people blind to truth, and who would do anything to silence the voice of Islam. Barakah stood by him, unshaken."

---

tradition, these birds dropped stones of baked clay upon the invaders, serving as a miraculous sign of divine protection over the Sacred House.

Voices of a veiled age

I stare at the floor. Faith, what a strange and tangled word, how hard it is to carry something in your heart and stand by it.

"Now turn so I can braid your hair."

Silently, I turn my back to Hababeh. I feel like a little girl surrendering herself to her grandmother's hands.

Truly, if a person has a mother or grandmother like Hababeh, it is as if an army stands beside them, a great and ever-victorious army.

"Life holds many sweets and many bitters, ups and downs, hard and sorrowful days and days full of joy and celebration. Having someone by your side through all of that is no small thing. Many share your joys but not your sorrows. Barakah was one of those rare souls; she never let her heart stray from the Prophet's family. After Lady Khadijah, even though she became a mother herself, she still cared for Lady Fatima ﷺ. The Prophet's daughter spoke freely to Barakah; at times, Barakah was her steady rock, at times the keeper of her secret. Alongside all that love and tenderness, she carried the courage of a lion."

She parts my hair and begins to braid. The scent of her hands lingers in my hair, and it soothes me.

I shift, and Hababeh mutters, "Do not move, dear girl. I don't want to give you back a crooked braid."

I ask, "You still haven't told me about Barakah's bravery."

"Yes," she says. "Many things happened in the house of the Prophet ﷺ and Lady Fatima ﷺ. Angels often visited, though few ever knew of it. Barakah was all eyes and ears; she kept the Prophet's words in her heart, took Lady Fatima's words ﷺ to heart, and whenever she was among the women, she spoke of the heavenly message. Through her, many women of Mecca turned to the Prophet's faith. Barakeh always knew what to say and when, though her own heart remained a locked chest of secrets."

She pauses. "Turn back, Zubayda. It`s done. I tied the ends beneath the weave with a thread from my headscarf for you."

I turn and look at her trembling, wrinkled hands. Barakah knew what to say, what to do, and so do I. Waiting is hard, and so is bearing the heavy air of this palace. The sound of the Iranian girl's fervent recitation rings in my ear: *'perhaps you dislike something, yet it is good for you'*[8] I believe in the God who made those words shine in His Prophet's ﷺ heart. I must fight this crushing state without pause.

I am no Siyana to see molten copper as a garden of roses. I am not Sumaya to cry out my faith aloud under torture. I am not Qanwa to stand unbent in oppression. I am not Umm Khalid, whose courage and discretion were the talk of gatherings. I am not Barakah, who gave her life to the Prophet's family. I… I am like none of them. Yet I am burned, torn limb from limb, cast to every wind in hope of rescue, of rest, of balm. After my Imam's martyrdom, only ash remains, waiting to be scattered by the gentlest breeze.

"Zubayda, my child," Hababeh's voice brings me back.

"Your sad eyes make my heart tremble. Take my last words into your soul: this family is light. Set a lit candle in the palace courtyard, and many insects gather. Some will stay at a distance, others will be utterly captivated, offering themselves to the light. That is the grace. This burning, this falling apart, this turning to ash, it is itself birth."

It feels like she can see right through my tear-blurred eyes, easing the ache in my chest.

---

[8]Surah Al-Baqarah -2:216

Voices of a veiled age

"I wish I could keep you with me forever," I whisper.

"You are not meant to stay here, Zubayda," she answers softly

"I cannot bear this poisoned air of the palace. I do not want to see Harun's wicked face again. But where could I go? I do not know."

"Sometimes leaving holds a good that staying never will. Sometimes you must go. I saved Barakah's story for last, because it is a story of leaving. When Barakah's hair turned silver, all of Mecca called her Umm Ayman, after her son Ayman. Though her childhood and old age were rooted in Mecca, one day she chose to leave."

"Why? She who loved the Prophet and his daughter so fiercely, how could she leave?"

"It was that very love that made her go. Courage and devotion welled up in Umm Ayman. When war came, and the Prophet ﷺ rode out, she could not bear Fatima's ﷺ restlessness. She put on armour and entered the battlefield like a warrior. None of the women you have heard of stood as Umm Ayman did, placing herself in the path of danger for the Prophet's sake, yet never wavering. At the Battle of Uhud, she stepped forward, ready to make her chest a shield for the Prophet's ﷺ life."

I had never imagined myself taking up a sword and going to battle. My fixed stare at my hands makes Hababeh laugh. "What are you thinking, my dear? You were never meant to wield a sword. Umm Ayman didn't either. The Prophet ﷺ forbade it. But she was determined to go and would not leave the Prophet ﷺ and the Muslim army, so he entrusted her with another task, an important duty."

I place my hand beneath my chin. "What duty was that?"

"She carried water to the soldiers and cared for the wounded. At one moment, she slung a waterskin over her shoulder to quench parched throats; at another, she dressed wounds and wiped away blood, all the while keeping her eyes on the Messenger of God ﷺ, lest…"

Hababeh's voice trembles. She falls silent, leaving her words unfinished. Her shoulders shake, and suddenly she breaks into sobs. Surprised, I place my hand gently on her shoulder. When she spoke of Sumaya's and Siyana's brutal tortures, or the loneliness of Qanwa and Umm Khalid, she had not wept like this. I draw her head close to my chest.

"What happened so suddenly? Why have you broken down like this?"

Hababeh trembles, weaker now, and her tears soak through my clothes, chilling my skin. I run my hand over her thinning hair, trying to calm her. Between broken sobs, she whispers, "The next time we meet, I will be as Umm Ayman once was. That day, you will be there and so will Siyana, Sumaya, Qanwa, Umm Khalid, and Umm Ayman. One moment, we'll carry water to the fighters, the next, we'll bind their wounds. The only difference is that the Prophet ﷺ will not be with us, and in his place…"

I draw back; my face flushed with heat.

"What are you saying, Hababeh? Speak the truth. By God, am I to see those who died long ago, whose bones have long since turned to dust? Why spin such fancies? Why pull me toward madness?"

With tearful eyes, she gives me a sorrowful smile. "The call to prayer is near. My journey is close. I must finish Umm Ayman's story, and then you will have your answer."

I rise, agitated, slip on my sandals, bite my lip, and go to Henna, who is awake and watching me. When she sees me, she lowers her head. I slip my hand into the cage and scratch her neck. A faint sound rises from her throat and fades.

Hababeh says, "The Prophet ﷺ, like all human beings on this earth, closed his eyes to the world. After that, Umm Ayman stayed closer to Fatima ﷺ than ever. In the hardest days of life, her presence showed itself more than ever before. Oh, the heart of Fatima ﷺ, the jewel of the Messenger. Oh, her bleeding heart. Fadak was at the height of her loneliness."

I nod. She continues, "Fadak was the rightful property of Fatima Zahra ﷺ, but it was taken away from her. When Fatima ﷺ went to claim it, Umm Ayman stood by her side. That day, she showed the full measure of her courage and devotion. A council had gathered, men unmatched in debate and speech, their brows furrowed and chests swelling with anger toward Ali's family. Hardly anyone dared to stand against them. No one expected anyone to oppose the council. But Umm Ayman was not like the rest. She spoke out, sweeping their arrogance aside. She believed her only purpose in the world was to defend the Family of the Cloak[9]. You know the council ruled that Fadak did not belong to Fatima ﷺ."

"Yes, I know. I've heard it."

Hababeh glances at the Henna. "After the ruling, Umm Ayman could not remain still. She raised her voice, defending Fatima ﷺ and Ali ﷺ with a force that no man in history had ever shown such courage.

---

[9] Family of the Cloak (Ahl al-Kisā'): The five holy figures gathered under the Prophet Muhammad's cloak during the Event of the Cloak: the Prophet himself, his daughter Fatima, his cousin and son-in-law Ali, and his grandsons Hasan and Husain. In Shia tradition, the Family of the Cloak represents the core of the Prophet's purified household (Ahl al-Bayt), distinguished by their spiritual authority, moral perfection, and divine selection.

Voices of a veiled age

My dear, the injustice against Ali's ﷻ family began from the beginning. After the Prophet's ﷺ passing, their isolation only grew deeper. Those who hungered for wealth and power turned away. Anyone close to the Prophet's ﷺ children was treated as an outcast, as if they deserved mistreatment. But Umm Ayman raised her voice for the truth. She spoke of the Prophet's birth, his mission, and the event of Ghadir[10], and when she came to Fatima's ﷻ suffering, her voice burned with anger."

My eyelids flutter. I rub my eyes, and she goes on.

"They demanded that Fatima ﷻ bring a witness for Fadak. Barakah stepped forward; she had seen the Prophet ﷺ give it to his daughter. But the men of Medina rejected her testimony simply because she was a woman. Barakah turned to the caliphs and cried, 'O God, these men have wronged Your Prophet's daughter, bring Your punishment upon them!' Can you imagine the courage it took to speak those words?"

Ghadir, Fadak, the Prophet's daughter, injustice, rights, the caliphs, Harun...the words whirl inside my head. If, on the day of the Prophet's death, justice had been restored and Ali ﷻ had taken his rightful seat of power, everything would have been different. Perhaps today I would be studying at the feet of Musa ibn Jafar ﷻ. A soft sigh catches in my throat.

Hababeh murmurs, "Fatima ﷻ did not live long after the Fadak dispute; she could not endure the pain of being apart from her father."

---

[10] Ghadir (Event of Ghadir Khumm): The historic event in 632 CE where the Prophet Muhammad, during his return from the Farewell Pilgrimage, publicly declared Imam 'Ali ibn Abi Talib as his successor and the leader (mawlā) of the believers. Held at a place called Ghadir Khumm, this declaration is central to Shia belief in the Imamate and is commemorated annually as Eid al-Ghadir.

Voices of a veiled age

Days had passed since the burial of Ali's wife. In Medina, the air grew heavy for Umm Ayman, almost suffocating.

Each glance at Fatima's ﷺ house pierced her heart, and the tears came unbidden. She decided to leave Medina and go to Mecca. For her, the journey was a way to draw nearer to her beloved.

"Perhaps this is the path you should take," she said. "Leaving this palace will give you peace, Zubayda."

"I know, Hababeh. But where can I go?"

She came closer, squeezed my hand.

"You must go where no memories can follow you. Then your heart will find calm, and you will become yourself again. Distance can make unspoken things rise and be heard. After leaving, Umm Ayman devoted her life to worship and service.

In Mecca, she spoke of the Prophet ﷺ , of Ali ﷺ and Fatima ﷺ; her tears dried, her heart finally found rest. Sometimes distance is the best pain medicine."

I close my eyes for a moment.

"I wish I had another life to devote entirely to the Ahl al-Bayt. I wish time could turn back, and I might have struck Harun before the martyrdom of Musa ibn Jafar ﷺ."

"God will grant you another life," she replied.

The certainty in her voice makes me restless. I pull my hand away from hers.

"Hababeh, where do you find such hope? Harun, that wolf-hearted tyrant, martyred our Imam ﷺ, and now he schemes against his son… Yet you speak as if you had lived among those women. You cannot know their hearts as I do."

A broad smile lit up her face. "I am nothing like you, Zubayda. God knows, except for Siyana, I've met the others closely at most once. I told you, I came all this way to see you, the seventh wife, my child. Have you forgotten?"

I ease the cramp in my side and walk toward the curtain. "What do these stories have to do with me? Isn't it time you answered the questions that have been gnawing at me since the evening? You claim you've seen those women. how? Don't tell me you're related to the Prophet Noah. Your years don't stretch back that far."

She falls silent, and her silence gnaws at me. I twist my ring for the hundredth time, bite my lip, and step back. A storm simmers inside me. I halt in front of her, studying the delicate lines on her brow.

"Speak, Hababeh. My heart is restless."

She lifts her head, and I sink into the wet depths of her eyes. "My daughter, baseless distrust comes from the devil. Do you think I lied? Or deceived you? That is nothing. But from all I have lived, as one with white hair who has seen two hundred and fifty-three years, take this one truth to heart: never trade your afterlife for the feeling pleasures of this world."

I whisper, "Did I hear that right? Two hundred and fifty-three years?!"

She moves to the bed and pulls her robe over her head. "Yes. My long life was a gift from my Imam ﷺ. Zubayda, when the descendants of Ali wills something, legends themselves take on the colour of truth before them. If they will it, miracles can unfold in the blink of an eye. Do you want answers? Then listen. God had granted me 111 years of life. I was old, frail, hunched, my hands trembling. After the martyrdom of Husain ibn Ali ﷺ, I set out to find Imam Sajjad ﷺ. Factions had multiplied, and everyone claimed to be a ruler or an avenger. I had to bring the marker stone to the Imam ﷺ, so that his seal could bear witness for those who searched for a sign. And so I went. Limping, I presented myself before the Imam ﷺ. His servant brought me water and asked me to wait. I leaned back against a cushion. The Imam's house had inner rooms, and from the next chamber came muffled sounds: prayers, perhaps a recitation. I became restless. That day, I had none of the patience I carry today. Hours slipped by. I pressed myself against the wall, unable to stand straight. Slowly, I dragged myself into the next room. There he was, radiant like the sun, bowed in prostration, unaware of my presence. I gently pushed the door open and crouched in the corner. I forgot why I had come, forgot my exhaustion. I just sat there, watching him bow and prostrate, every part of his being immersed in prayer. His beautiful voice brushed against my ears, while the fragrance of his perfume filled the air around me. His beautiful voice brushed against my ears, while the fragrance of his perfume filled the air around me. Tears slipped down my face. He looked like my first Imam ﷺ. Gradually, my tears dried up. After all, one is only human, and we grow weary so quickly. I shifted to ease the pain in my bones. Time passed. I could not tell how long. At last, words escaped my lips: 'My master, my strength is gone; have mercy on my old age. I am weak, and I wish your prayer would come to an end.' Zubayda, the very moment I spoke, it felt as though the Imam himself bent into ruku with me. My words breathed new life into my soul. What happened to Zuleikha happened to me as well. A miracle unfolded before my eyes."

Voices of a veiled age

She breaks into sobs, trembling. I hold her to my chest. Am I asleep? Awake? My God... what a night this is. Hababeh still weeps like a child, trembling as she cries. I gently stroke her back.

"You have become young. Colour has returned to your hair, flesh to your bones, light to your eyes. Your skin is clear. Have you been granted a second life? Can such a thing be? Hababeh, be still."

She lifts her head, her eyes red and raw, tries to speak but chokes, pressing a handkerchief to her mouth. Blood blooms across the cloth, staining it red. Fear rises within me. I lead her toward the bed, but she refuses to sit. I start to speak, but she lifts her hand to silence me.

"Listen, my daughter. I have asked nothing of you. I want nothing. You may doubt my words, call me a deceitful old woman, or say I am mad. But know this, from all I have lived, from me whose hair has turned white, who has walked this earth for two hundred and fifty-three years, accept this: I have come to tell you a secret. With it, you may choose with a calm heart and full certainty. Your choice can make your life flourish your life in this world and the next. Not only yours, but it can touch hundreds, quenching dead hearts like water. And if you doubt me, when I am gone, send someone to ask about me, and about the women whose names you have heard. I want you to know that you can be the voice of the Shia who languish unjustly in Harun's prisons. You can be the voice of the Imam ﷺ who was killed by poisoned dates, while your husband dressed his lifeless body in new clothes, combed his hair, laid him on a fine mat, and showed him to the people, saying, 'Look, he died a natural death; we treated him with kindness.'"

My eyelid trembles; my head feels heavy, my stomach turns. Hababeh is right; Harun truly did that. He ordered Sindi to kill the Imam ﷺ in prison, but afterwards, they brought his body to the palace, laid him on a bed, and claimed he had died a natural death. How I wept and wailed in those days, crying and striking myself against the walls.

I pleaded with Harun again and again to let me see the Imam ﷺ, and he refused. I endured the decree, but I could no longer bear to see him martyred in such a way. After his martyrdom, I did not leave my room for three days. My hair turned white, hope fled from my eyes, and a tremor at the corner of my eye began that day and has never left me. I was a lost soul who wished to speak to no one. Looking back now, I see that my cries and tears made Harun suspect my Shi'ism, and perhaps that was for the best, for tonight, at sunset, I was called to account."

I squeeze Hababeh's trembling hands.

"By the One and Only God, I would give my life for my faith. I never wish to hear Harun's name uttered beside mine. Do not leave your words half-said."

A sudden knock at the door breaks my words apart. Hababeh and I turn toward the door. Haniya steps inside. "Why are you awake? Has the call to prayer started?" I ask.

"Yes, my lady. I couldn't sleep. God knows my body feels torn apart tonight. The adhan is near. We must take this old woman out of the palace. I've spoken with Muslim. When the guards change in a few minutes, it will be the perfect time for her to leave."

I sink back onto the bed. Hababeh nods to Haniya and draws her robe tighter around her head. Henna calls out, "Zubayda, Zubayda!" I glance at her, twisting my ring between my fingers.

Hababeh rests her hand on my shoulder. "What troubles you, my daughter?"

Voices of a veiled age

My head feels as heavy as stone. I lift my eyes to her. Can she truly bear two hundred and fifty-three years upon her shoulders? Haniya steps closer, and I say, "Haniya, pack a small bundle, just what you truly need."

"My lady…"

"Go, Haniya. There's no time."

I have to hurry. I have to listen to my heart. I have to be myself. Hababeh kneels before me and lays her hand gently on my knees.

"The time has come for you to know the deepest secret. But first, tell me what Harun and his vizier did to that girl who went into the Imam's ﷺ prison to dance, and came out a Shia?"

I place my hand over her wrinkled ones.

"They wanted to behead her, but I helped her get away. I still have friends who stand by me."

Her smile softens. "Good. Then I can rest easy. Ask those same friends for help. You built the Zubayda Well in Mecca and saved the Shia more than once, so you can surely protect yourself."

"Since the martyrdom of Musa ibn Jafar ﷺ, death no longer frightens me."

"I know. Tonight I've come to know you truly. Do you remember saying you wished to see Siyana or the other five women? You said you longed for another life, one you could give entirely to the People of the House."

I nod silently.

"I promise you, one day you'll see them. You may not realise it, but if you choose, you already belong among those women. Your life, mine, and theirs are woven together. I'm certain that somewhere in time, we'll

Voices of a veiled age

meet again. Believe me, Zubayda. One day, we will return to this world and stand in the ranks of our Imam."

Her words are hazy yet sharp, cutting straight through me.

"It all began the day I went to Imam Jafar al-Sadiq's ﷺ house to ease my longing for him. The Imam ﷺ was teaching his students. I listened quietly from behind the door to his words. He spoke of the Saviour, the end of time, and the last son of Ali ﷺ who would fill the earth with light. One of his students asked if only prophets and saints would stand beside him. The Imam ﷺ paused, then said, 'No. Both women and men will be with the Imam.' With my own ears, I heard him name seven women: 'Qanwa, daughter of Rushayd al-Hajari; Umm Ayman, known as Barakah; Sumaya, mother of Ammar ibn Yasir; Umm Khalid; Siyana, the hairdresser; and Zubayda bint Jafar.'"[11]

Tears stream down my cheeks. My tongue is tied, my body trembling like Hababeh's.

"Me? Am I truly one of the companions of the Imam of the Age? Oh my God…"

Hababeh gently presses a soft kiss on my forehead. "Yes, my daughter. The words of God's friend are true. There is no doubt. Know your worth and your value. You are a Shia descendant of Ali ﷺ. This is your honour. Do not hide it. If you remain silent, who will awaken the sleepers and ask why the Prophet's son was bound? Once, power belonged to Pharaoh and Nimrod; now it rests with the Abbasids. My

---

[11] For the narration attributed to Imam Jaʿfar al-Ṣādiq mentioning Qanwa bint Rushayd, Umm Ayman (Barakah), Sumayya, Umm Khalid, Siyanah, and Zubayda bint Jaʿfar, see: Al-Quṭb al-Rāwandī, Saʿīd ibn Hibat Allāh. al-Kharāʾij waʾl-Jarāʾiḥ. Qum: Muʾassasat Imām al-Mahdī, n.d.; also cited in: Al-Majlisī, Muḥammad Bāqir. Biḥār al-Anwār, vol. 47. Beirut: Dār Iḥyāʾ al-Turāth al-ʿArabī, 1983.

child, what bears no sign of truth, even if its towers reach the sky, will come to ruin."

I cannot yet grasp Hababeh's secret. I stand there, stunned. "Please, speak to me," I whisper.

"Zubayda, my dear," she answers, "your name is inscribed among the ranks of the Imam of the Age. You must act. let your faith and devotion shine. Remember this always: the true caliphate is like the sun; by its light, we live. Without that light, we have nothing. Nothing at all."

I rub my tired eyes. Tears have traced lines from my lashes down to my chin. I do not know what to ask or say. My mouth feels frozen, my fingers numb. Hababeh smiles softly, her expression calm and comforting. She reaches for her sash. Haniya stands by the door with a bundle. I wipe away my tears and fix my gaze on Hababeh.

She carefully takes out a white embroidered cloth, unfolds it, and lifts the signet stone. She folds the cloth and holds it toward me. "This cloth has held the signet stone safely for many years. It is my cherished keepsake for you."

She presses the cloth to my face and its scent is sweet. I swallow my sob and squeeze her hands tightly. Slowly, with a trembling voice, I say, "Hababeh, please take Haniya with you. She will accompany you on this journey. Money and jewels matter little to you, but this girl is precious to me, and from now on she will care for you."

Hababeh nods and smiles. Haniya's chin trembles; I know she cannot bear the parting. But I cannot let Hababeh go to Medina alone in her fragile condition. I release Hababeh's hands and fold Haniya into my arms. Her shoulders tremble. I gently pry her away, wipe her tears, and say,

"Care for her as you would your own soul. Love her as you would love me."

She nods obediently, her face trembling. I turn back to Hababeh. "Your words have stuck to me like bread to the oven, lodged in my heart like an arrow of light. I wish I could see you again, I wish…"

Hababeh drapes her headscarf around her face; only her eyes remain visible, and they look young.

"Answer my last question, Hababeh. You said you heard seven names, but only spoke six. Who is the seventh?"

"Muslim is at the door. It's getting late, my lady…" Haniya murmurs.

Hababeh draws me close. I breathe in her sweet scent. She squeezes my hands, then, a peculiar light in her eyes, walks toward Haniya with a serene, floating step. I hear her whisper,

"We will meet again on the promised day, beside the Qa'im of Muhammad's[12] house. Until then, farewell."

The door closes. I kneel in the center of the room, pressing the cloth to my face as sobs escape me. Hababeh's perfume lingers in the air. And so, the story begins.

---

[12] Qa'im of Muhammad's Household (al-Qā'im min Āl Muḥammad):
A title in Shia tradition referring to the divinely appointed, rising Imam who will stand to establish justice, truth, and divine governance on earth. Most commonly used as a title for the Twelfth Imam, al-Mahdi (may God hasten his reappearance), "al-Qā'im" literally means "the One Who Rises," signifying his role in overturning oppression and restoring the path of the Prophet and his purified Household.

Voices of a veiled age

Voices of a veiled age

7

Life gives humans a short window of opportunity. A short window that people often see as longer than it is. Perhaps that is why they make wrong decisions. Perhaps they do not realise that this brief time is the only chance to choose, to shape an entire lifetime. I chose at one point in my life, just a week ago, and my choice was real. I chose to open my eyes and stand before a man whose hands are stained with the blood of the descendants of Ali ﷺ. Now, sitting here in this damp, dark pit they call a prison, where every few moments the scuttle of a rat shakes me to my core, I feel lighter than I have ever felt.

When Hababeh left, I was left alone, bombarded by thoughts that pierced me like triple-headed arrows. Hababeh's secret was strange and astonishing to me. I had never considered it before, and I did not think I deserved it.

Voices of a veiled age

That day, after she and Haniya left, I heard the footsteps of the guards outside my room as soon as dawn broke. I had been crouching on the floor when they opened the door and peeked inside. Harun was not with them. The vizier searched everywhere for Hababeh and could not find her. He ground his teeth and spat beside Henna's cage, glaring at me with eyes full of warning. Nothing mattered to me. I wanted to get out of the vast palace that felt to me like a dark, cramped dungeon as quickly as possible. As soon as they left, I called for Nira. No one could be Haniya for me, but I had to trust her. Nira was a servant who worked in the kitchen. She had an uncle who was a Shia. I had learned this during the first days after she arrived at the palace and began reciting the Quran. I asked her to go to her uncle as often as needed and return with an answer to my question. Hababeh had penetrated my heart, and I believed her words, but a small flicker of doubt sometimes flared in my mind. Doubt about whether I would also be among the women of the army of the Awaited Imam. Even though staying in the palace felt like torture and bearing the title "Harun's wife" was unbearable, I closed the door on myself and sent a message asking for a few weeks' grace. Amin managed to get Harun to grant me this time. Harun, thinking I would reflect in private and then, like before, become Lady Zubayda, agreed.

Every day, the servants stood at the door with trays of food. Every few days, I opened the door for them, taking bread and a bowl of yogurt. In the privacy of my room, I went over Hababeh's words not just once, but a hundred times. I savoured them, her kind eyes, her heartfelt and straightforward speech. Then I thought of Sumaya's resistance, Qanwa's faith, Siyana's bravery, Umm Khalid's stubbornness, and Umm Ayman's love. Hababeh's voice repeated constantly in my mind: "Do not sell your afterlife for the pleasures of this world, Zubayda. This family is light."

Hababeh had told me that on the night of the Mi'raj, when the Prophet ﷺ journeyed to the heavens, a fragrance filled his soul, one unlike anything he had ever known. Gabriel had told him that the scent came from the bodies of Siyana and her children, who had been burned in molten copper, and that their fragrance would drift through Paradise for as long as the world endured.[13]

Hababeh had said that when Sumaya writhed under torture, when the sun scorched her skin and her head burned with fever, the Prophet sat beside her and said, "Your place is in Paradise."

Hababeh had said that whenever the Prophet ﷺ saw Umm Ayman, his heart overflowed with joy. He would smile and say, "This woman is my mother, and she is among the women of Paradise."

Hababeh had said that whenever Imam Sadiq ؑ saw Umm Khalid, he invited her to his gathering and asked her to narrate hadiths.

Hababeh had said so much. I don't know how many days passed, five, a week, maybe several. It was just me, the room, my prayer rug, and the Quran. I went over Hababeh's words again and again, regretted the deeds I had left undone, and wept for the martyrdom of my oppressed Imam. Then Nira returned. She said her uncle had confirmed the authenticity of Imam Sadiq's ؑ narration. She brought with her a piece of parchment on which the text of the hadith had been inscribed. Seeing

---

[13] This narration appears in Shia and Sunni Mi'rāj traditions. For the Shia version, see: al-Majlisī, Biḥār al-Anwār, vol. 18, pp. 90–91, which records Gabriel telling the Prophet that the fragrance he smelled during the Mi'rāj came from Māshita (Siyāna) and her children, martyred in molten copper. A parallel narration is also found in Musnad Aḥmad (ḥadīths 27525–27526) and in the Mi'rāj accounts of Ṣaḥīḥ Muslim.

Hababeh's name beside mine and the five other women's put an end to all my doubts. I opened the door to the people of the palace. The first to come was Amin, my handsome, noble son, in whom I had never hoped to find an Alawi's heart. Amin tried everything to make me speak, but I remained silent. I had promised myself that I would not utter a word except before Harun.

At last, a week ago, the vizier came for me with a group of soldiers. It was time to speak. When I stepped out of my room, the women were standing in the palace hall, watching me. I turned my eyes away from them and fixed my gaze on Harun's chamber door. I lifted my head and walked in. The same men who had questioned me just hours before Hababeh's visit were there. Harun reclined against a saffron-coloured cushion, holding a new rosary of red sandalwood beads. His thin gold-embroidered cloak was drawn over his legs. His brows were furrowed as he stared at a half-naked girl twisting and swaying before him like a beautiful snake, the hem of her skirt swirling in the air. Another girl played music while she danced. I threw a faint, bitter smile at the dancer's slim waist. She was beautiful, beautiful and alluring, but when your heart is heavy, beauty loses its light. That day, in that moment, everything looked dim and broken to me. Every bit of luxury in Harun's room felt like a thorn in my eyes. The vases full of red and yellow flowers stirred nothing in me. The little monkey swinging in its cage could not make me smile. Even the jade basin, filled with clear water where two graceful swans glided and bathed, something I had once watched for hours, no longer caught my attention. My eyes were fixed on Harun. He had cut his hair short, and the reddish dye on his beard made my stomach turn. He was uneasy, and I could feel it clearly. He said nothing, and I poured all my hatred into my gaze. When the weight of my gaze unsettled him, he gestured for me to take some of the grapes from the platter. My eyes moved over the ruby clusters, the dried figs, the sweet almond pastries that used to be my favourite. Harun bent forward and grabbed a handful of seeds. The girl's music had stopped; the only sound in the room was the crack of the seeds between his sharp teeth. Now that I think back, I realise I felt nothing at that moment. I thought I had already experienced every feeling there was, and nothing new could touch me anymore. When I didn't move closer and kept my eyes fixed on him instead of the grapes, he finally looked at me. His eyes seemed softer, yet there was something new in them, something I couldn't name. It was as if Harun stood at a crossroads, just like when he had hesitated before ordering the arrest of the Imam ﷺ, or when he had struggled to give the command for his death. A faint smile played on his lips, but I could see the restlessness in his eyes, perhaps even the glimmer of tears. It was that same hesitation, those wrong choices, that dragged Harun to the depths of ruin. Sometimes I think he knew he was wrong, but he lacked the courage to admit it, or perhaps he could not let go of his crown and throne.

That day, he pointed for me to come closer. I obeyed. He tapped the arm of his wooden throne with his ring, and a servant filled his cup. He loved his throne more than his own life. It was a two-seated masterpiece carved with peacocks and lions, the frame gilded in gold, the lion's mane and the peacock's feathers inlaid with silver, rubies, and emeralds. Two saffron cushions rested on the throne, one for Harun and the other for me. Of course, that second cushion had been mine only until the Imam's martyrdom. Harun drained his cup of wine in one long swallow and

Voices of a veiled age

wiped his lips with his sleeve. His voice rose sharply. "We all believe you've turned Rafidi," he said. "You were eager to see Musa ibn Jafar, and after his death, you fell ill. You've done plenty to help the Rafidis, and worst of all, you let that old woman escape against my command. Now I have only one question for you, Zubayda. What is your faith? Do you still follow our creed?"

A bead of sweat slid down the middle of my back, but I didn't look away from his eyes. I twisted my turquoise ring around my finger. The corner of my eye kept twitching, again and again, maddeningly. I wanted to shout that I had nothing to say to the killer of Zahra's son, but I bit down on my teeth instead. I whispered *Bismillah* and, before the watching eyes of Harun and the men around him, I spoke. "You are right," I said. "I am a Shia, a follower of Ali ibn Abi Talib ﷺ."

The room exploded in uproar. Voices overlapped and clashed. The twin girls, terrified, grabbed their instruments and fled the room. Someone in the crowd shouted, "The traitor's fate is the sword." He was right to say so; Harun never spared a traitor. He wanted every soul in the palace to know what became of those whose hearts beat for the descendants of Ali ﷺ.

But I was ready. I had no fear of the blade or the gallows. I placed myself in the stead of Sumaya, of Qanwa, of Siyana.

That day, I expected Harun's men to rush at me on his command. I expected the executioner to enter, to unroll his leather mat across the floor. But Harun raised his hand, and the room fell silent. The pupils of his eyes were wider than ever, his face redder than the day he killed Abasseh, even redder than the day he sat beside the Imam's body while Sandi told him they carried the coffin over the Baghdad bridge to show everyone he had died naturally. Yet the Imam's cold white lips moved, and facing the onlookers, he said, "They have killed me."

Harun was like molten metal, burning red. His hands trembled, and I could clearly see the flaring of his nostrils. I watched him twist like a poisoned man. I waited for him to speak, and he half-stood and shouted, "By the one and only God, I divorce you. I give you three divorces!" I laughed. He thought this was the worst punishment he could give me. To Harun, love meant control. He wanted an obedient slave, a Zubayda who would give up her beliefs without question, bow before the Caliph, and live her life like a sheep.

I do not know where the words came from that day, but a tear fell from my eye as I whispered, "During the days I was your wife, I hoped with my womanly power to keep your hands from being stained by the blood of Fatima's children. But I could not. I feel no love for you. I will remain a Shia."

Harun threw the cup from his hand onto the ground. It shattered into a hundred pieces, like my heart. He shouted louder than before, "I do not recognise you anymore. You are not Zubayda. I never want to see your face again."

Beginnings behind every ending are as astonishing as they are inevitable. They are inevitable because the world never stands still; it moves on, whether we want it to or not. They are astonishing, because within them we discover another self, a new version of who we are. After I walked out of Harun's chamber, for the first time, I felt a quiet sense of satisfaction, satisfaction with my own choice.

I went back to my room to pack my belongings. The thought of where to go and what to do wouldn't leave me. I kept whispering under my breath, "O my God, grant me the perfection of turning wholly toward You." It was at that very moment that the message arrived. Harun had ordered that I leave everything behind and move to a small house in Baghdad. Going there was like entering a prison. Harun had not arrested me in words, but in truth, he was sending me into captivity. Accepting that was hard, but I promised myself I would search for light among pain, sorrow, and hardship, like the saddest yet most hopeful seeker of gold, and this time, I would devote my whole being to the descendants of Ali ﷺ.

I tied up my bundle, said farewell to my maids who recited the Quran, took Henna's cage in my hands, and was about to leave the palace forever when Haniya returned with the news of Hababeh's death. Grief washed over me again.

◆

Henna's voice calling my name, "Zubayda, Zubayda," pulls me back to the present. I push the memories aside. The cold stones of the prison floor seep into my bones. I stretch my folded knees, but there's no space; the dungeon is too narrow, and they remain bent. Henna's cries grow louder. Maybe her seeds are gone, or her water. Or maybe she just wants me to scratch her head and play with her. Slowly, I rise, my stiff body lifting painfully from the ground, and I call out, "Haniya, Haniya, come here!"

She feels her way toward me in the dark. My eyes have grown used to the blackness. She carries Henna's cage in her hands and my bundle tucked under her arm.

Voices of a veiled age

I stop a few steps away from her. She turns her head, trying to take in the darkness of the dungeon. "How did Musa ibn Jafar ﷺ survive a whole year in this absolute darkness? Hababeh was right to mourn for him in secret and weep."

I smile. She has every reason to speak of Hababeh that way. I spent one night with her, but Haniya had been her companion for days.

"Tell me about Hababeh," I say. "What happened after you left the palace?"

I can hear the fear in her trembling voice. She glances toward the prison door and speaks softly. "That day, Muslim had cleared the path. The guards were either gone or among his friends. I left the palace and, near the mosque, a caravan was preparing to depart. It was headed for Medina. The leader knew Hababeh and looked at me with anger. Hababeh explained that I was with her. I wanted to pay for both of us with the money you had given me, but Hababeh wouldn't allow it."

She unties a cloth belt around her waist and took out three small pouches. "Except for a few coins I used on my way back, all the money you gave me went untouched."

That was just like Hababeh. She had shown her generosity that very night.

"So, nothing happened on the road?" I ask.

"Not really," she says. "I kept fearing the palace guards would come after us, but nothing happened. Only, the closer we got to Medina, the worse Hababeh became. Every cough she had was filled with blood."

She gradually stopped eating and could take nothing but milk.

I step forward and take Henna's cage from her. Henna calls out, "Zubayda, Zubayda!"

"Tell me, Haniya," I ask. "When did you bring the stone to Ali ibn Musa al-Ridha ﷺ?"

I don't know what will happen next, but Haniya bursts into tears, her whole body shaking.

"What is it, my child?" I ask.

"I wish I hadn't come. I wish I had stayed there. You spoke the Imam's ﷺ name, and it made me miss him so much."

I place my hand gently on her shoulder, surprised.

"You saw the Imam ﷺ?"

"Just once, and from afar. But he smiled at me."

"Where? Haniya, please, tell me. I'm desperate to hear."

Haniya wipes her nose and swallows back her sobs. "As soon as I reached Medina, Hababeh's son took us to his house. Hababeh had become so small, just skin and bones. I stayed by her side all night, worried for her. Her daughter-in-law stayed with me, too. That same night, she told me Hababeh's story."

"What story? Tell me. What do you know about Hababeh?"

"Hababeh's daughter-in-law was her niece. She said that Hababeh's father had died when she was a child, and a few years later, her mother had died of leprosy. At that time, Hababeh had been so young."

But because her sisters and only brother were younger than her, she had to work. Spinning was Hababeh's trade. She worked from dawn until late at night, caring for her sisters and brother, and then through the night she tended to her mother.

Lady, her daughter-in-law, said no one dared to come near Hababeh's mother. Everyone was afraid the leprosy might spread to them. But Hababeh would bring her food, speak to her, and help her however she could. This went on for many years. Hababeh's mother grew old and frail, while Hababeh became a young woman.

A man came to ask for her hand, a man who seemed pious and devout. She pauses and glances at the prison entrance.

"Why are you silent? Keep going."

"I'm afraid the caliph's soldiers will arrive, Lady."

I take Henna's cage from her hands.

"They are after me, not you. You are not in danger. Now continue. Did Hababeh marry?"

Haniya sniffs and goes on. "Yes, she married, hoping to lighten some of her burdens. But her marriage brought its own hardships. Her daughter-in-law said Hababeh's husband was a hypocrite. Outwardly, he appeared devout, maintaining ties with the Prophet and Imam Ali, but his true plan was to send information to the enemies of their family. Hababeh discovered the truth quickly. She confronted her husband, but all she received in return were slaps, kicks, and imprisonment. Her husband, afraid that Hababeh would expose him, locked her in, even though she was three months pregnant at the time."

My heart aches, and my temples throb. Hababeh, why didn't you speak of yourself? Why did you hear all the words of my heart and say nothing of your own sorrows?

"How many years did she live with her husband?" I ask.

"For many years, Lady. Even when Hababeh's mother died, her husband only allowed her to leave the house to say goodbye to the body. I think her son was seventeen when her husband died. Her daughter-in-law said that when Hababeh, who was my aunt, came to our house after her husband's death, her whole body was bruised, her hip broken, and her arms covered in scars. After that, Hababeh returned to spinning, raised her son with care, and with her brother's help, built a home."

I remember her sweet smiles and her fearless, gentle eyes. Life had been hard for Hababeh, hard and exhausting. Yet she had fought to preserve her faith.

Haniya's voice pulls me back from my thoughts. "There is one more thing, Lady. Her daughter-in-law said that many years ago, Hababeh gathered women in the city square and spoke to them about the right of the descendants of Ali. She cursed the ruling government and urged the people to think of the Hereafter."

She falls silent again. "Haniya, aren't you going to speak?"

I feel the lump in her voice. "Yes, Lady. But whenever I think of Hababeh, I start crying for no reason." I take her hand in mine.

Her daughter-in-law said, "After that sermon in the square, they took Hababeh to prison. God knows what tortures she endured. Her daughter-in-law only told me about her nails being pulled out, but that is not the whole story. A few weeks later, when Hababeh was released, she tried to return home, only to find there was no home waiting for her. They had burned her house along with all her belongings."

My knees go weak, and now I feel tears welling up, too. I let go of Haniya's hand. "Is that why she lived in her son's house?"

"Yes, Lady. She had nowhere else. That night, her daughter-in-law and I talked until the call to prayer. Hababeh woke at the prayer, and as soon as dawn broke, she put on her travelling clothes. She said I had to stay at home. No matter how much I insisted, she would not let me go with her. Her daughter-in-law said not to push her, for Hababeh always did what she wanted."

Voices of a veiled age

I nod. She knew what she had to do, and she knew what she wanted from life. "Was she well when she left? Did she go to serve the Imam?" Haniya takes a deep breath and continues, "She was better than the day before. I was unworthy not to go with her. At the time, I didn't know where she was going. When she returned, her face was glowing, and her cheeks had regained colour. Her son came and showed us the stone, the one stamped with Ali ibn Musa al-Ridha's ﷺ seal. It was the same stone she had shown you in the hallway when she arrived. That's when I realised she had gone to serve the Imam ﷺ."

Haniya begins to cry again, her trembling voice echoing through the prison walls. "She talked to me almost until morning, about her childhood and her youth. But she never spoke of her husband, never mentioned her hardships. Mostly, she spoke about the descendants of Ali ﷺ and asked me to stand by them for as long as I live. I don't know when it happened or how I fell asleep. I wish I hadn't. I wish…"

"Don't cry, Haniya. It wasn't your fault."

"Maybe… I don't know. If I had stayed awake, maybe we could have called a doctor."

I squeeze her shoulder. "A doctor couldn't have done anything."

"When I opened my eyes in the morning," she says softly, "I saw her lying on her side, facing the qibla. Her face looked hollow, her cheekbones sharp. Her mouth was slightly open, and her eyes were closed. She had placed the sealed stone on her chest. I screamed and cried. Her daughter-in-law came, then her son. The house filled with people. Her son was restless, trying to arrange the funeral, when something happened."

"What happened?"

Haniya lifts her head. Her eyes have now adjusted to the darkness, and she looks straight at me.

"The Imam ﷺ had sent word that he himself would come to perform the burial."

Jealousy, awe, sorrow, I cannot tell what it is, but my heart tightens painfully. Hababeh, how blessed you were.

"They carried her body to the mosque," Haniya continues. "I followed them, running. There, I saw the Imam ﷺ. How can I tell you, my lady, in a way that you would believe me?"

It was sweeter than anything in the world, even sweeter than seeing Muslim. Before that day, whenever I saw Muslim, my heart would race and my hands would tremble. But that day, it was not only my heart; my whole being trembled, and tears fell freely from my eyes. The Imam ﷺ wrapped Hababeh in his own shirt and led the prayer over her. I saw him only from afar. By God, if it had been up to me, I would never have gone back to Baghdad. I would have become a servant in Hababeh's daughter-in-law's house, just to stay near the Imam ﷺ.

Her words do not surprise me. She has fallen in love, and this is what true love is. Love is a divine gift, and heavenly love is not granted to everyone. Haniya is touched by grace.

"I wish you had stayed," I tell her softly.

"I couldn't. Hababeh made me swear to deliver a message to you."

My brows knit together. I bite my lip. "What message? Why didn't you tell me sooner?"

"The palace was in such chaos," she says, her voice trembling, "and seeing you shook me so deeply that I couldn't speak. Forgive me."

"Tell me now," I whisper. "Tell me what Hababeh said."

Voices of a veiled age

"That night," Haniya says, her eyes glistening, "the night before she didn't wake up, she told me, 'After I die, go to Zubayda and tell her this: Now that you are light as air, now that the chains have fallen from your wings and the cage lies broken, fly toward the light.'"

"That was all?"

"Yes," she says softly.

I stare at her, speechless. Something stirs inside me, awakening in every part of my body. We are fragments of the past, pieces of the present, and echoes of the future. Time is not a line; it is a sphere, with no beginning and no end. Wherever you stand within it can be both a starting point and an ending. I had planned to leave this prison and go to the small house Harun had given me. That was supposed to be the end of my story. But Hababeh's message, it is the beginning. I must go. I must rise.

I turn my eyes away from Haniyah, my chin trembles. I bend down and pick up a flat, small stone from the corner of the dark cell. I press it to my lips. Then I pull from my waist the embroidered cloth Hababeh had given me as a gift and wrap the stone inside. The stone feels sacred in my hands. Perhaps the Imam once rested his forehead upon it. Perhaps his blessed hand brushed against it. Perhaps even the dust beneath his feet has touched its surface.

"We have to go," I say, my voice trembling but firm. "Hurry, Haniya."

"What is it, my lady? Where are we going? To the house, the Caliph promised?"

I tighten my fist around the stone. A thin beam of light falls across my face. I quicken my pace and start climbing the steps. Sometimes we have to break so that our crooked bones can heal properly, this time. We must

Voices of a veiled age

not fear a broken heart if the healer is skilful, if we are patient. The one who heals the bones of my heart is the most skilful of all. I smile, and a single tear rolls down my cheek.

Haniya repeats her question. I stop on the last step, my eyes fixed on the sun. Its light pierces my vision as I whisper, "We are going to Medina."

Bibliography

Zubayda bint Ja'far

Ṭabarī, Muḥammad ibn Jarīr. *Dalāʾil al-Imāmah*. Qum: Muʾassasat al-Baʿthah, 1st ed., 1413 AH.

Kaḥḥālah, ʿUmar Riḍā. *Aʿlām al-Nisāʾ fī ʿĀlam al-ʿArab wa'l-Islām*. Beirut: Dār Ṣādir, 1892 CE.

Ibn al-Athīr, ʿAlī ibn Muḥammad. *al-Kāmil fī al-Tārīkh*. Beirut: Dār al-Fikr, 1398 AH.

Ibn al-Jawzī; Ibn Khaldūn; Ibn Khallikān; Ibn Ṭiqṭaqā. *al-Fakhrī fī al-Ādāb al-Sulṭāniyyah wa'l-Duwal al-Islāmiyyah*.

ʿAbd Allāh al-Māmaqānī. *Tanqīḥ al-Maqāl fī ʿIlm al-Rijāl*. Qum: Muʾassasat Āl al-Bayt (ʿalayhim al-salām) li-Iḥyāʾ al-Turāth.

Ibn Qutaybah al-Dīnawarī, Muḥammad ibn ʿAbd Allāh ibn Muslim. *al-Maʿārif*. Qum: Manshūrāt al-Sharīf al-Raḍī.

Aʿlamī Ḥāʾirī, Muḥammad Ḥusayn. *Tarājim Aʿlām al-Nisāʾ*. Beirut: Muʾassasat al-Aʿlamī li'l-Maṭbūʿāt, 1408 AH.

Ḥusayn, Qadriyyah. *Shahīrāt al-Nisāʾ fī al-ʿĀlam al-Islāmī*. Beirut: Dār al-Kitāb al-ʿArabī.

Yaʿqūbī, Aḥmad ibn Abī Yaʿqūb. *Tārīkh al-Yaʿqūbī*, vol. 2, p. 429.

Jaʿfarī, Jawād. *Bānūwān-e Rajʿat-Kunandah*. Qum: Bunyād-e Farhangī-ye Ḥaḍrat Mahdī Mawʿūd (ʿajjal Allāh taʿālā farajahu al-sharīf), 1392 SH.

Ṭabāsī, Najm al-Dīn. *Chashm-Andāzī beh Ḥukūmat-e Ḥaḍrat Mahdī (ʿaj)*. Qum: Bustān-e Kitāb.

Nūrūzī, Zahrā. "Ḥayāt-e Siyāsī wa Ijtimāʿī-ye Zubayda Khātūn." *Majallah-ye Tārīkh-e Islām* 19 (1383 SH).

Pīshvāyī, Mahdī. *Sīrat-e Pīshvāyān*. Tehran: Intishārāt-e ʿImād, 1380 SH.

Sumayya bint Khayyāṭ

Ṭabarī, Muḥammad ibn Jarīr. *Dalāʾil al-Imāmah*. Qum: Muʾassasat al-Baʿthah, 1413 AH.

Ibn al-Athīr, ʿIzz al-Dīn. *al-Kāmil fī al-Tārīkh*, trans. Muḥammad Ḥusayn Rūḥānī. Tehran: Asāṭīr, 1370 SH.

Ibn al-Athīr, ʿIzz al-Dīn. *Usd al-Ghābah fī Maʿrifat al-Ṣaḥābah*. Beirut: Dār al-Kutub al-ʿIlmiyyah, 1418 AH.

Ibn Hishām, ʿAbd al-Malik ibn Hishām. *Sīrat Ibn Hishām*. Beirut: Dār al-Maʿrifah.

Amīn, Sayyid Muḥsin. *Aʿyān al-Shīʿah*. Beirut: Dār al-Taʿāruf.

Sharaf al-Dīn, Ṣadr al-Dīn. *ʿAmmār ibn Yāsir: Pioneer of Islam and Standard-Bearer of ʿAlī (ʿa)*, trans. Sayyid Ghulām Riḍā Saʿīdī. Tehran: Āʾīn-e Jaʿfarī.

Subḥānī, Jaʿfar. *Farāz-hāʾī az Tārīkh-e Payāmbar-e Islām*. Tehran: Daftar-e Nashr-e Farhang-e Islāmī, 1371 SH.

Qummī, Shaykh ʿAbbās. *Muntahā al-Āmāl*. Qum: Nashr-e Dalīl, 1379 SH.

Majlisī, Muḥammad Bāqir. *Biḥār al-Anwār*, ed. Muḥammad Bāqir Maḥmūdī. Beirut: Dār Iḥyāʾ al-Turāth al-ʿArabī, 1403 AH.

Qanwāʾ bint Rushayd al-Ḥijrī

Ṭabarī, Muḥammad ibn Jarīr. *Dalāʾil al-Imāmah*. Qum: Muʾassasat al-Baʿthah, 1413 AH.

Qummī, Shaykh ʿAbbās. *Safīnat al-Biḥār wa Madīnat al-Ḥikam waʾl-Āthār*. Mashhad: Āstān Quds Raḍawī, 1388 SH.

Amīn, Sayyid Muḥsin. *Aʿyān al-Shīʿah*. Beirut: Dār al-Taʿāruf.

Majlisī, Muḥammad Bāqir. *Biḥār al-Anwār*. Beirut: Dār Iḥyā᾽ al-Turāth al-ʿArabī, 1440 AH.

Barakah bint Thaʿlabah (Umm Ayman)

Ṭabarī, Muḥammad ibn Jarīr. *Dalāʾil al-Imāmah*. Qum: Muʾassasat al-Baʿthah, 1413 AH.

Ibn al-Athīr, ʿAlī ibn Muḥammad. *Usd al-Ghābah fī Maʿrifat al-Ṣaḥābah*. Beirut: Dār al-Fikr, 1409 AH.

al-Mufīd, Muḥammad ibn Muḥammad. *al-Ikhtiṣāṣ*. Proceedings of the Millennium Conference of Shaykh al-Mufīd, 1413 AH.

Ibn Abī al-Ḥadīd. *Sharḥ Nahj al-Balāghah*, ed. Muḥammad Abū al-Faḍl Ibrāhīm. Beirut: Dār Iḥyāʾ al-Kutub al-ʿArabiyyah, 1378 AH.

Ibn Ḥajar al-ʿAsqalānī, Aḥmad ibn ʿAlī. *al-Iṣābah fī Tamyīz al-Ṣaḥābah*, vol. 8. Beirut: Dār al-Kutub al-ʿIlmiyyah, 1415 AH.

Ibn Saʿd, Muḥammad ibn Saʿd. *al-Ṭabaqāt al-Kubrā*. Beirut: Dār Ṣādir, 1405 AH.

al-Balādhurī, Aḥmad. *Ansāb al-Ashrāf*, ed. Muḥammad Ḥamīdullāh. Cairo, 1959 CE.

al-Ṭabarānī, Sulaymān ibn Aḥmad. *al-Muʿjam al-Kabīr*. Cairo, 1404 AH.

Ṣiyānah al-Māshiṭah (The Hairdresser of Pharaoh's Daughter)

Ṭabarī, Muḥammad ibn Jarīr. *Dalāʾil al-Imāmah*. Qum: Muʾassasat al-Baʿthah, 1413 AH.

Jazāʾirī, Niʿmat Allāh. *al-Nūr al-Mubīn fī Qiṣaṣ al-Anbiyāʾ waʾl-Mursalīn*. Qum: Maktabat Āyat Allāh Marʿashī Najafī, 1404 AH.

Majlisī, Muḥammad Bāqir. *Ḥayāt al-Qulūb*. Qum: Surūr, 1384 SH.

Maḥallātī, Dhabīḥ Allāh. *Rayāḥīn al-Sharīʿah fī Tarjamat Banāt al-ʿUlamāʾ al-Shīʿah*. Tehran: Dār al-Kutub al-Islāmiyyah.

Umm Khālid al-Maqṭūʿat al-Yad

Ṭabarī, Muḥammad ibn Jarīr. *Dalāʾil al-Imāmah*. Qum: Muʾassasat al-Baʿthah, 1413 AH.

al-Kashshī, Muḥammad ibn ʿUmar. *Rijāl al-Kashshī*. Qum: Muʾassasat Āl al-Bayt (ʿalayhim al-salām), 1363 SH.

al-Kulaynī, Muḥammad ibn Yaʿqūb. *al-Kāfī*. Tehran: Dār al-Kutub al-Islāmiyyah, 1407 AH.

al-Khūʾī, Abū al-Qāsim. *Muʿjam Rijāl al-Ḥadīth*. Qum: Muʾassasat al-Khūʾī al-Islāmiyyah, 1409 AH.

Ḥabābah al-Wālibiyyah

Ṭabarī, Muḥammad ibn Jarīr. *Dalāʾil al-Imāmah*. Qum: Muʾassasat al-Baʿthah, 1413 AH.

Ibn Bābawayh (al-Ṣadūq). *Man Lā Yaḥḍuruhu al-Faqīh*. Beirut, 1401 AH.

al-Kulaynī, Muḥammad ibn Yaʿqūb. *al-Kāfī*. Tehran: Dār al-Kutub al-Islāmiyyah, 1363 SH.

Ibn Shahr Āshūb. *Manāqib Āl Abī Ṭālib*. Qum.

al-Ṭūsī, Muḥammad ibn al-Ḥasan. *Rijāl al-Ṭūsī*. Qum, 1415 AH.

al-Ṭūsī, Muḥammad ibn al-Ḥasan. *al-Ghaybah*. Qum: Muʾassasat al-Maʿārif al-Islāmiyyah.

Maḥallātī, Dhabīḥ Allāh. *Rayāḥīn al-Sharīʿah*. Tehran, 1370 SH.

www.ingramcontent.com/pod-product-compliance
Lightning Source LLC
Chambersburg PA
CBHW020412080526
44584CB00014B/1285